SINDI G.

WO MAN'S VIEW FROM A PORTHOLE

WRITE
CONTACT

Seattle, Washington, USA

SINDI GIANCOLI

WOMAN'S VIEW FROM A PORTHOLE

www.WomansViewFromAPorthole.com

Published by Write Contact
www.WriteContact.com

Book design by Sonja L. Gerard

Front cover design by Sonja L. Gerard
Back cover painting of the ship Saga Sea by Don Kotts, RIP.

Printed in the United States of America.
Paperbound edition of this book originally printed by:
Ingram Spark/Ingram Content Group, One Ingram Blvd., La Vergne, TN 37086
www.ingramspark.com

ISBN 978-0-578-33880-4 (pb)

10 9 8 7 6 5 4 3 2 1

This book is dedicated to my fearless, beautiful daughter, Shana.
I hope she carries what she learned from me into the world,
finding love, strength, conviction, and self-reliance in every horizon
she chooses to follow and every storm she overcomes.

/ Author Sindi Giancoli with Sigurd Johnny "Sig" Hansen /

FOREWARD

BY SIG HANSEN

I think the public will enjoy reading Sindi's book because it is coming from a woman's point of view. The truth is any book that's written from a female perspective about Alaska or Alaska fisheries is going to show something unique. It brings the other side of the coin to the plate. Also, Sindi is speaking about long ago. She was truly living in a man's world. By seeing it through a female's eyes, she really opens the reality as to what was going on. In the man's world back then in Alaska, it was like living in the Wild West. So, in my memory, it's almost as though when you left Seattle, you were going into a whole different world. So, seeing something, anything, from a woman's perspective during that time is quite interesting because in the pecking order, then and now, men seemed to rule the roost. They/we were and are there for one reason, and one reason only – to make money. It's an animalistic lifestyle.

I would imagine coming from a woman's point of view, that's about as black and white as you can get. The contrast is probably such that the guys don't care. You're in our world. So, the priorities are different. I can imagine it would probably be one of the hardest things for any female to do.

Segueing to my daughter, Mandy, I sympathize with her and women like Sindi who have struggled to survive in a male industry that is driven by ego, testosterone and an "anything goes" attitude. My hat's off to them – and at the same time, I don't wish that on any woman and/or person.

Everyone wears a different hat at home than they do at sea. You come home. You have your children. You have your family. But when you're at sea, and this goes for anybody at sea, you must be a different person, change personalities and suck it up for the job. But if you're a "go-getter" on land, you'll also instinctively be a "go-getter" on sea. That attitude translates. That's the kind of person who will make it in the waters of Alaska in the Bering Sea. Let me put it in plain words. There is no Human Resources in the fishing industry in the Bering Sea. You must roll up your sleeves. If you don't have a thick skin, you need to get the hell out. So, it takes a special woman, or person, to work in fisheries. You'll find out quickly if you're suited to this type of industry or livelihood. Nine-to-five is out the window and it takes someone who cannot just take it but can also dish it out. You must stand your ground, especially if you're a woman in any Alaska fishery.

On a personal level, I've known Sindi for many years. At home, Sindi's always been forthright, she's a go-getter, she's always the one who makes things happen and she's the first to say, "do you need help with anything." People like Sindi are far and few between, especially now, because in today's day and age we have a very sensitive, younger political population that don't always seem to fit the bill. So, what I appreciate, and respect are people like Sindi who've been there and done that with a little more "old-school" mentality – and, after generations, can still bring it.

Sigurd Johnny "Sig" Hansen is an American captain of the fishing vessel *Northwestern*. Since 2006, he has been featured in every season of the documentary television series "Deadliest Catch," serving as technical advisor for the production. He is also author of the book, *North by Northwestern: A Seafaring Family on Deadly Alaskan Waters*, available through Barnes and Noble. He and his wife, June, live in the Ballard district of Seattle, Washington.

CONTENTS

INTRODUCTION

In July 1990 when I boarded the brand-new Norwegian fishing trawler, *Saga Sea*, in Tacoma, Washington, I could have never guessed what the next twenty-eight years would bring to me. Little did I know the enormous adventures that were ahead or where my hard work and diligence would lead. All I knew was that I was scared to death. I'd been hired to work as a galley assistant and had never cooked in a restaurant. The only cooking experience I'd ever had was cooking for my children as a "mom cook" and a little time working in a deli. I had no idea how I was going to make it work. But, as an alcoholic who was by then two years sober, I'd faced adversity before, and not only survived, but been victorious. Through sheer tenacity I'd beat the odds. How could working on a fishing vessel be any harder than that ordeal? I knew I wanted an exciting life and to travel. Plus, as a single mom, I needed a job that paid well. Working in commercial fishing, I'd be adventuring on the high seas while making a living. What better way to see the world than from the deck of a fishing vessel? So, I left my family and friends behind on the shores of the Puget Sound and embarked on what would become an astounding, life-changing experience.

This book is the story of how I went from a galley assistant to Chief Steward, an accomplishment seldom achieved by anyone, much less a woman. Working as a steward in commercial fishing would become my life's work. For readers who might not know, a chief steward is a senior crew member who, on a fishing vessel, serves the same function as a manager in a restaurant. Considered an officer, as Chief Steward, I planned menus and provided oversight for meal preparation and serving, food ordering, cooking and baking. I also facilitated budgets, directed and provided training for all steward's assistants, and managed ship maintenance and inventory in all departments. All this, while tossing around on the high seas.

It was a true adventure. But it was also risky. Despite recent technological advances, commercial fishing today is still considered one the most occupationally dangerous jobs in the world. In the 1990s, it was even more so. A good third of the people I worked with are no longer alive. Despite the dangers, from the first moment I stepped on the deck of the

Saga Sea and felt that surge of anticipation to this day, I've never tired of those blue, white-capped waves stretching far into the horizon, or their salt spray splashing against the portholes. Looking back, I know serving on a commercial fishing vessel is where I was meant to be.

Through multiple trials, tribulations, joys, sorrows, and struggles, I went from a scared, timid young woman to a woman of achievement, confidence and strength in an industry that was, and to a certain extent still is, primarily male-dominated. Being contained on a fishing vessel at sea is, I imagine, a lot like being in prison. You live with, eat, sleep, work, confront, and connect with the same people day after day. These people, in some ways, know you better than those closest to you on land. Together, you survive high seas, gale-force winds, seasickness, illnesses, death of crewmates, stress, homesickness, bunking together, broken toilets, power outages, hauling fish, food fights, and getting along, despite your wildly diverse cultures and backgrounds.

Being one of a few women on a fishing boat was highly challenging, particularly once I became head of a department. I had to build a strong backbone and win the respect of my male counterparts while leading them. This was a very slippery slope, on which I constantly teetered between discouragement and resilience. In addition to these challenges aboard, I gave up a lot on land to live the fishing life. I missed birthdays, holidays, births and deaths of friends and relatives. I slept in rugged, sometimes inhospitable conditions. I suffered a lot of sexual harassment and mistreatment. I was completely alone and sometimes felt lonely.

But, what I was able to accomplish during the years I worked on fishing vessels was a far cry from the terrified young woman who had hesitantly boarded the *Saga Sea* in the early 1990s. I became a part of what would be termed years later as "a very special generation of women" who claimed ownership of our work at sea. We were tough and resilient. I discovered I had inner perseverance and a gut level will to not only survive but succeed under unimaginable circumstances. In the spirit of my story, it's my best hope that by sharing it other woman are encouraged to face their challenges head-on, and by doing so, find their own adventurous rewards in life.

SECTION ONE:
ABOARD
THE *SAGA SEA*

SWAN FISHERIES, INC.

GALLEY ASSISTANT

AUGUST 01, 1990 - OCTOBER 11, 1990

DECEMBER 25, 1990 - FEBRUARY 04, 1991

Boarding the
Fishing Vessel *Saga Sea*

My hands nervously clutched a small, blue ditty bag I'd bought at a small fisherman's store in Ballard, Washington. Slung over my shoulder, it carried everything I would wear for the next three months. Had I remembered to bring lip balm and sunscreen? Did I pack my heavy fleece sweatshirt and windbreaker? Did I remember my new deck shoes? I'd just arrived at the Port of Tacoma, Washington. I was headed north to Alaska and had no idea what kind of weather I might encounter. I just knew that I'd been instructed by a very firm male voice, Don Kotts of Human Resources, to pack lightly and not bring a suitcase since storage space was limited on the ship. He'd told me if I did bring a suitcase, it would be thrown overboard. So, not wanting to test this edict, I'd dutifully packed everything into one compact bag. For some inexplicable reason, he'd also told me to leave any plush toys at home. Norwegians had a superstition about having them aboard, and I was told if I brought one, it would also be thrown overboard. I had, however, packed a photo of my beloved Pekinese, Sophie. Photos would be my only reminder of home, and these were allowed. Despite the bag's diminutive size, my slim, stalwart body sweat in the weight of it, causing perspiration to roll down my face and neck. July in the Puget Sound is the only time of year hot weather hits Seattle and by Pacific Northwest standards, at 70 degrees that day in 1990, it was only a mildly hot day. But for Puget Sound residents, anything above 65 degrees is hot, particularly since I was weighted down by an extra heavy jacket. I was sweltering.

It was July 31, 1990. Two years before, I'd decided to make a huge change in my life. I'd stopped drinking. During that time, I'd met a woman, Phyllis, who had been a true friend and supported my sobriety. It was Phyllis who suggested I apply for a job at her company. When I asked what she was doing, she said she did housekeeping on the fishing boat, *Claymore Sea*. Initially, I'd planned to go to work on her vessel as a fish processor, but then the plan had fallen through. That's when Don Kotts (RIP) had called me and offered me an alternative, to work on the *Saga Sea*. Paul Halvorson, my cousin, was president of the company and a boat broker but that had no bearing on my hire. Boats that fished in U.S. waters had to have a certain percentage of American steel in their construction. So, to comply with this regulation, Paul would buy boats in the U.S. that needed to be refurbished and send them to Norway. However, Paul's work was completely unrelated to why I was offered my job. Rather, Don had noticed I'd worked in a small store with a food deli, and deciding I had food experience, suggested I should work as a gallery assistant on a brand-new vessel their company had coming in from Norway, the *Saga Sea*. He had no idea I was related to Paul. At the time, in fact, I had no idea what Paul's job was either. I'd immediately said yes, which was why I was now standing in Port of Tacoma waiting to board a commercial fishing boat.

As I looked around at my surroundings, I noticed the seaport, Port of Tacoma, Washington, teamed with activity. Huge container ships, with company names scribed across their port (left) sides, lay like sleepy giants across the wide spans of water, stilled before carrying cargo to destinations all over the world. I'd heard the Port of Tacoma marine cargo operations were among the largest in the United States. Measured against this statistic, I felt even smaller as I waited for someone to show up and tell me what to do next. My family had left me on the dock. Phyllis stayed with me for moral support. I was so scared. As a kid, I'd climbed aboard my family's cabin cruisers. So, I wasn't a total stranger to boating and the water. However, I'd never been aboard anything as large as the *Saga Sea*. Anxious, I craned my neck to look up at the massive ship that would soon be my home away from home. Feeling a twinge of homesickness, I'd said goodbye to my friends and family to go on this adventure. It had been especially hard to leave my dad, who was in the hospital at the time. But he and his wife, Helen, had encouraged me to go. Had I done the right thing? I looked up. The *Saga Sea* loomed above me. At nearly 319 feet long, she was imposing and impressive. It gave me some comfort to know that she was built as a safe boat, with a keel like a sailboat that enabled her to withstand heavy swells. With a 60-degree listing ability, the likelihood she'd flip over in a storm and not be able to right herself was slight. Her steel bow gleamed white in the sun, stretching stately across the water. The air around me smelled pungent and salty. Seagulls called to each other in the sky. White clouds drifted high above the horizon. I felt my twinge of angst begin to melt into excitement.

The dock under me rocked slightly with the wake of ships moving into port. I braced myself, legs spread slightly apart, a stance that would become all too familiar once I was out to sea "getting my sea legs." It had been a long time, two years to be exact, since my body rocked like this, and that was only after a night of binge drinking. I could hear my AA sponsor's words echo in my mind, "Be careful, Sindi, there's a lot of drinking aboard fishing vessels. It's part of the culture." But drinking was not going to be an option for me. I didn't want to start something I knew I couldn't finish, and drinking was a sure-fire way of ensuring I would fail. Without sobriety, I knew eventually I'd go insane. With God's help and meditation, I was determined to keep my mind sharp and my head sober. I knew that boarding this vessel and taking the job as a galley assistant, however, was an essential part of my recovery. I was carrying the solid belief that I could get through anything and succeed. I was also aware the fishing industry was mostly a man's world, which I suspected might be problematical. Commercial fishing at one time been exclusively a man's domain, including unabashed carousing and heavy partying. As a woman, I knew I'd probably face occasional push-back from some of my male counterparts simply because I was a woman. However, nothing was going to derail me. I'd come too far to stop now.

As I looked around, I saw a group of men who would become my crewmates sitting on the docks. Half had already been aboard and were waiting to re-board, but we would have to wait for what seemed to me to be an interminably long period of time. As I came closer, I heard some of them speaking in a language I presumed was Norwegian. I'd been told that 20 of the crew were Norwegian and 20 were American. During those early days of fishing, all my crewmates who fished were Norwegian. The Americans held other jobs, like fish processors or sorters. It would be years before I would discover that Americans also fished or even knew how to fish. Commercial fishing vessels operating in Alaskan waters were usually based and hired out of Seattle.

Restless and hungry, we all waited together on the dock. Apparently, U.S. Customs had boarded the vessel with drug dogs to clear it for departure. This routine inspection, which was the first of what would be many during my commercial fishing career, delayed our boarding of the *Saga Sea* by nearly two hours.

Finally, after what felt like an eternity, we boarded the vessel up a long gangplank and gathered in the *Saga Sea* galley, a large, state-of-the-art stainless-steel galley boasting new equipment. It was impressive by anyone's standards. Everything shone with the crispness of a freshly built boat. A five-foot marble baker's table stretched along one wall, while stacked convection ovens hung against another. Steam kettles cozied into railed stoves. Stainless steel mixing bowls stacked against one corner and a hanging whisk the size of a small baseball bat hung with an array of over-sized metal mixing spoons. Clearly this was a galley made for some serious cooking. While everyone else was being shown the duties they would perform aboard, I was introduced to my boss and Chief Steward, John Bloomfield, and to the galley and responsibilities he would expect of me. To say John liked to party would be an understatement. He was an amicable guy and we got along great, but he also liked to smoke pot and was an alcoholic, albeit a friendly one. Even his morning coffee had scotch in it. I would learn quickly that this laissez faire attitude toward smoke and drink was very common aboard. At the end of every workday, John and the purser, Marcy, would always imbibe in "Happy Hour" in the galley.

Another crew mate was fired and put ashore for drinking, but John and Marcy relished sneaking alcohol anyway and getting drunk together. The sight of them hammered would become a familiar one. I'd often catch John in the walk-in refrigerator stealing a nip or two. John would also buy box wine and have me cover it with a cloth in the galley, serving it to him surreptitiously. The Norwegian officers who came through the food line also expected the same. I always felt work on a boat was challenging enough when I was sober that I couldn't imagine adding alcohol to my already rocking body. I was glad the captains I crewed for stayed away from alcohol while on board. For one, the Coast Guard forbad drinking alcohol of any kind while driving the boat. If a Captain was caught drinking, he'd lose his license. Plus, there were multiple variables the Captain had to keep track of, such as water depth, submerged trees and rocks, and size and direction of waves. On a fishing vessel, there were added dangers too, such as the large, potentially lethal equipment. However, John was only "Captain of the Galley," and he loved his brew. But that first day when he met me, he was all business.

After a very quick orientation, John told me I'd be assisting him in feeding one hundred people in the mess hall that day. Yes, just the two of us. Much to my dismay, I realized this meant I'd be single-handedly washing one hundred plates, knives, forks, and spoons. It was quite a job!

After we had served a meal of white fish in a cream sauce, mixed green vegetables, a side of whole grain bread, and dessert of chocolate pudding to everyone, I cleaned the galley. I'd only been aboard 12-hours. Already every bone in my body ached, and we hadn't even left port yet. I was relieved to learn this serving expectation would alter to only 50 people twice a day after we left port and headed north to Alaska. I'd also continue to have John's help along with the assistance of a First Cook. But, as I was soon to discover, cooking on a moving vessel out to sea is much more challenging than cooking in a kitchen at home. Everything lists and bounces when the boat heels over during swells of 10 to 15-feet or more or when it hits a sudden wake, including the food you're cooking and serving. I learned to be very agile.

That first day, though, since we were waiting for supplies, we stayed anchored in port, where we would remain for the next week. I was pleased to see two people aboard from AA. I knew one of them had been fishing for 5 ½ years and the other had four years of sobriety, so it wasn't a surprise. However, sadly they'd both slipped off their programs. One had started drinking again, but had now been sober for 60 days, while the other was still trying to get back on his program. Seeing them furthered my own resolve to stay sober.

As I walked around the vessel, *Saga Sea* was every bit as beautiful and awe-inspiring inside as it was outside. She'd just arrived from Norway, where she'd been converted into a fishing vessel, accounting for why half of our crew was Norwegian. They'd come over from Norway with the vessel. That was fine with me. I counted myself lucky to be among them. Since *Saga Sea* was on her maiden voyage from the shipyard, she was sparkling clean. She was a state-of-the-art fishing vessel ready to welcome her first crew aboard. We'd be discovering Alaska and the Pollock fishing industry together.

Saga Sea was the last of her kind to be built abroad. Under the Jones Act of America Fisheries, federal requirements stated that vessels had to be owned by U.S. companies with at least 75 percent U.S. ownership, registered in the U.S. This is how the U.S. company, Emerald Resource Management, was formed as a holding company for Swan Fisheries that "owned" *Saga Sea*. When the boat had hit the dock in July, I was the only crew who hadn't already been on board for a month. At the time, I had a boyfriend who was a sheet metal fabricator and built products for fishing boats. My knowledge of the fishing industry and commercial fishing vessels was limited to what I'd learned from watching him fabricate pieces for boats. I knew factory fishing vessels went to sea for weeks on end and during that time processed huge catch in giant freezer holds below, but I had no idea how the fish was processed before it was frozen. I also had no restaurant or cooking experience. You could say I was a fish out of water in more ways than one.

As I climbed the narrow gangway up to the boat's lower deck and worked my way down the hall with anticipation toward my tiny wooden bunk room, I caught a quick glimpse of the officers' mess where the officers would be eating. A few of them, looking far too pressed for fishing, were talking about our upcoming departure. With its padded leather seating, wide tables, and sizeable portholes, this area looked comfortable and inviting. In contrast, outside the officers' mess was a long, narrow, metal mess hall for the rest of the crew. Set up cafeteria-style for efficiency and quick meals, it was already noisy with clanking dishes. In the days ahead, I'd be serving a lot of food in both places.

Smiling a shy greeting to other crew as I trudged down the semi-darkened hallway, I finally found my bunk room. I pushed my bag into a small gym-style locker and collapsed on the upper berth of a bunkbed. A musty, stagnant smell of seawater wafted through the room, but I was so tired, I didn't care. I collapsed on my berth and didn't wake until morning.

Rising at 7:00 a.m. and looking out a porthole, I could see dawn was beginning to break across the horizon, causing soft pink hues of light to rise and reflect on the water. I thought about what Phyllis had told me. She'd given me a vital piece of advice, which I still use to this day, and that was to take special care of chief engineers. "They will be your friends," she advised me, and if they liked me, they would reciprocate. I'd want them to support me when my stove broke. They'd fix it right away. I was looking forward to meeting them. Even though we were still in port and would be for the next week, looking out that porthole was my first taste of a view that would thrill my life for many years to come. It stopped my breath it was so stunning.

That day at 9:00 a.m., I went to work, and by work, I mean rigorous work. Everyone in the galley had left me to figure my way through the day on my own. My fear of failure was fierce, so I worked very hard to prove myself. I don't know if I've ever been so nervous or frightened. Every one of our supplies came on board, all at once – huge pallets of it. It was a zoo lifting all those heavy boxes of food and every supply the boat needed for the months we'd be out to sea Pollock fishing. That included the galley, bunks, heads, captain's quarters, and much more. I worked so long and hard loading food that day that my boss gave me permission to go ashore and check on my dad. Making the decision to leave and go fishing was hardest due to my worry about him. He was not any better, but to my relief, also not any worse. So, I made the decision, encouraged by my dad, to go ahead with my plans, however difficult it was to leave. That night, my 17-year-old daughter, Shana, cooked me dinner, reminding me of how blessed I was to have such a wonderful child who was so supportive of my choice to go fishing. On the other hand, Jenny, my goddaughter, clung on to me, weeping that she didn't want me to leave. It tore my heart out. I think she may have thought I'd never come back. But I promised her I would be back soon. My kids mean all the world to me. It was every bit as hard on me to leave them as it was for them to let me go.

Upon returning to the *Saga Sea*, we left Tacoma and went to Todd's Shipyard in Seattle (now Vigor Shipyards) for fuel. I was surprised to see my cousin, Paul, and his wife, Laurie, down on the pier. Along with a few other crewmates, I got off the boat for a short while. We met some people who drove us to a store and then back again to the dock. The boys wanted a six-pack, so we sat in a railroad yard and swapped "war stories." One of these guys was Tony, who would become my "little buddy" and show me the ropes in fishing. To this day, he is still a dear friend of mine. A few of the others were fish processors, which they related was a horrible, grueling job. Sorters pull fish off the deck and drop them into bins, where they're sorted by size. Sorters get covered in fish slime, shredded scales, and bile. But the pay was good, so they toughed it out.

A shipload of Koreans, Surimi tech specialists, boarded the *Saga Sea* to go to Alaska with us to oversee our Pollock Surimi production. They represented companies to which we sold product. Surimi, from the Japanese word meaning "formed fish," is often made from pollock. The pollock is gutted, washed, and run through a conveyer belt, where it is mechanically filleted by a BAADER food processor and washed again with cold water until it becomes colorless and flavorless. The fished pollock is processed into a gelatinous paste, packed and frozen aboard as raw material for further processing. This raw material is then shipped to Japan and Korea, where the crab-like pollock is reformed into various shapes, color, and flavor to resemble crab. The tech specialists spoke little English. Today, only a few specialists board the fishing vessels. Back then, however, they boarded by the shipload.

Before debarking and sailing to Alaska, the crew was also sent for training at the Sandpoint Naval Station in Seattle. This training was so monumental, it was featured on the Puget Sound's regional news broadcasts. It was the first time any kind of safety training had been done in the history of fishing and was an outgrowth of the many accidents and deaths at sea in the industry. Today, there are strict regulations surrounding safety and the fishing industry. But, back then, it was all but overlooked. To be quite honest, the fire drills frightened me, but I did take some comfort in knowing we were doing them.

My third day aboard, a high-pitched, shrieking noise shook me up. John instructed me to secure the galley with very little training about what that exactly meant. This made me extremely nervous. Once I felt I'd accomplished my task, I raced up to the wheelhouse all the while thinking, "What if this was a real fire? Would I be prepared?" Locating a stack of survival suits in the wheelhouse, I tossed them down to the Trawl Deck, where other crew members slipped them on. Emergency drills are critical on a fishing vessel because there are no outside emergency personnel on a boat. You're on your own until an emergency rescue helicopter, fire department, or medical professional arrives on the scene. So, it's very important all crewmembers know how to handle fires, as well as other emergencies such as man overboard and a sinking boat and know what each person is tasked with doing during one of these.

In the weeks, months, and years that followed, I never got used to the fire alarms. They would ring at any time of the day without warning. With very little training, I never was sure I was doing the right thing. Even more unnerving was when the boat would go suddenly dead without warning due to equipment failure. This seemed to happen a lot. It's so noisy on a fishing vessel that when the equipment's loud, grinding hum stops suddenly, the silence is startling. Ironically, this sudden quiet is deafening. The silence will wake you out of a deep sleep.

Once back on board, I had to switch from a two-man room to a six-man room, which meant I was to have limited privacy on the way to Alaska. Our room had previously been a hospital room, so it was well appointed with clean beds and good lighting. One of the women I was bunking with also worked in the galley. I don't think she liked me very much, despite the fact I was just trying to be helpful when I told her what to do.

My first day on the *Saga Sea*.

Dutch Harbor - The view from my porthole.

Phyllis, who introduced me to fishing.

Captain Kurt on the *Saga Sea*, my first captain.

Captain Bob of the *Saga Sea*.

Terri Shultz Mazza, a great friend and Chief Steward. I learned a lot from Terri.

American Seafoods
fleet, Pier 91,
Seattle, WA.

With Chief Engineer Dave Franca and Lorena, the housekeeper, on the *Saga Sea*.

Chief Steward Mike and Sindi taking a break on the *Saga Sea*.

View from a hotel window of Margaret Bay, Dutch Harbor, Alaska.

With "my little buddy, Tony," probably hiding from his bosses. Read his poem on the next page.

IN YOUR DREAMS

Somewhere in the distance
Waiting there for me
Is a place: a piece of mind
That's where I want to be
It's more than just a feeling
It's like something you just know
This little place inside your heart
You're just dying to go
- In your dreams -

Making memories
While futures are exposed
All through the centuries
While keeping both eyes closed
Black horses on white knights
Kings play and bishops ride
Illusionary sights are conjured up inside
Twisted and amused to confuse the open mind
When you look into your dreams
It's amazing what you'll find
Destiny oh won't you please
Tell me where you're taking me
Are you make or breaking me?
I guess I'll have to wait and see
- In your dreams -

- Tony Ramos

/ Peeling carrots for "potato ball day" on the *Saga Sea*. /

Aboard the *Saga Sea*

Peeking through the porthole as I lay stretched out my top bunk berth, a huge expanse of blue water spread out in front of me. I was glad I hadn't fallen out during the night, which had been one of my initial concerns. We'd weathered a wild storm the night before, with much rocking and rolling. But another morning was lapping across the horizon, calmer in daylight. The ocean, tipped in gleaming whitecaps, shimmered, with rivulets of light bouncing on its surface. Far enough out to sea to be out of sight of land, all I could see was a beautiful, flat landscape of blue stretching into the distance. I'd never seen so much open water. This was one of those even-keel, calm sea days I'd come to appreciate much more after I'd survived a few wild, unpredictable, dangerous storms at sea. Days like this one would become a welcome relief. But, today, all I knew was I had to get out of bed and didn't want to. Before leaving Port of Tacoma, we'd spent three days backloading pallets of food and supplies. My shoulders and back ached. My feet and ankles were swollen from the hundreds of meals I'd prepared, served, and cleaned for the past week, something that as the days wore on, I would begin to realize was just part of the job. I'd only been out to sea for three days and I was already body-sore and bone-tired exhausted. I'd worked so hard those first three days in the galley, in fact, that when the boat had pulled away from the dock and left the seaport, I hadn't even seen us leave land. Looking out the porthole window of my cabin now was the first time I truly realized I was far out to sea. I can't begin to say how daunting that was for me. I was scared to death.

Pulling myself reluctantly from my bed, I was relieved to see the shower stall was vacant. The *Saga Sea* had staggered our working hours so that the five other women I bunked with went to work at different hours than I did. This made for some relative privacy in the shower. It was somewhat fun taking a shower that day since the seas were high and we were being bounced around. I felt like I was in a circling Waring blender. Luckily, I've never had a problem with seasickness, something I would soon discover was not the luck of some of my other crew mates. After dousing myself with what turned to be a rather lukewarm shower, I threw on blue jeans, a red sweatshirt, and white-soled deck shoes. Dashing to the galley, I made it in the nick of time.

Also named Paul like my cousin, the *Saga Sea's* First Cook was waiting there to train me. Paul was my boss when John, the Chief Steward, wasn't around. Initially, Paul been very accommodating, helping me learn what I needed to do in the galley. But my experience with him quickly turned ugly. It was very puzzling and distressing. In fact, when he first yelled at me, I had to go outside to cry and collect myself. He went from being agreeable and helpful to agitated and altogether inhospitable. Initially, he'd pandered to me with assistance way beyond his job description. I was naïve enough to believe this overly expansive generosity was due to the fact he knew I was inexperienced and was just a guy who was being nice and wanted to help. As I've mentioned, I was a neophyte in more ways than one. Not only did I know nothing about cooking, I knew even less about the behavior of salty heterosexual men who'd been out to sea for months aboard a fishing vessel with nobody but other equally frustrated guys aboard. Paul, as it turned out, expected a lot more from me than he initially let on. His friendliness toward me rapidly turned into hostility as I thwarted his advances.

As a woman aboard, I would learn quickly that sex, with a few exceptions, would always be an expectation of me among my male crewmates. Sexual harassment was commonplace out to sea. No one monitored inappropriate behavior. Banter, inuendo, off-color jokes and teasing with intent ran a tenuous line between appropriate and over-the-line behavior. Weeks or even months could go by before we'd see land, so my crewmates improper conduct often compounded the longer we were offshore. I hadn't realized Paul's intentions toward me until one day he threw a stack of heavy pans on the deck and screamed at me, "I'm tired of helping you do your job. You do nothing for me!" That's when I realized his animosity toward me had everything to do with the fact that I didn't reciprocate his feelings, needs and desires. From then on, he made galley life miserable for me. I did dishes, and made salads, rice, and fruit dishes. I supplied crew with milk, juice and coffee. I swept, mopped, and catered to the cook's needs. Paul made sure I felt like his galley slave since sex was out of the question. He would bark orders at me incessantly.

To my relief, when I arrived at the galley that morning, my Chief Steward, John, was back in the galley. A nice man and a hard worker, he'd allowed me to take several breaks during the day. Since my shifts typically ran 12-16 hours a day, sitting outside on what I called the "galley lounge" was a solace for my sore feet. Crew on the *Saga Sea* typically worked 12-hour watches while underway or in port, and my job was no different. The galley lounge was a wonderful area with lounge chairs overlooking the ocean. On some days, I'd see pods of Pacific White-sided Dolphins following the boat, whistling to each other, diving and leaping through our wake. Stocky, with short, thick snouts, these playful creatures were about six feet long, weighing up to 400 pounds. Their grace in the water was spectacular. I've heard that dolphins probably surf the bow wave of boats simply because it's fun, and as social, intelligent creatures, they enjoy the company. It's also possible they like the boost of speed they get to help them get to their next feeding ground. Maybe, though, they recognized that our fishing vessel was headed to great sources of fish, so they were taking a ride alongside our bow to get fish for themselves. For, whatever reason, I never tired of watching these beautiful creatures frolicking through the water. This day, however, I was up on the bow, and to my surprise, saw a pod of Orcas, otherwise known as Killer Whales. Smart and strong, they were rearing up out of the water, their white underbellies glistening in the sun. Standing on the bow as salt spray splashed my face, I was struck with how lucky I was to be there, at that moment, watching those Orcas, unfettered in their ecstatic dipping and arching, fully alive and free. The view around me was breathtaking. I felt abundantly blessed.

The *Saga Sea* had already had three captains during her short time as a boat by the time I came aboard. Captain Frank brought her from Norway to Panama, followed by Captain Kurt, who brought the boat into Seattle.

Captain Frank was originally slated to take us to Alaska, but a family emergency changed his plans. We put him ashore aboard one of our skiffs, which are small raft-like boats usually tethered to the fishing vessel to help it navigate through rocky terrain.

Captain Dennis was our third Captain, a friendly, affable man who was comfortable with me going up to the wheelhouse. He'd stand stately amid a sparkling array of modern instruments and computers used to track fish, with a large, cylindrical metal wheel held in his sturdy, capable hands. I'd gaze past him, looking out the front window of the wheelhouse to the deck below. From that vantage point, I could see the *Saga Sea* stretched out, massive in front of me in all her regal splendor. A factory trawler, or fish processing vessel, she was built to operate fishing trawls, and process and freeze caught pollock in huge factories below her deck. Trawling is way of fishing that involves pulling a net through the water behind a fishing boat. The net, typically about 100 feet wide and 35-feet-high, is called a trawl and catches any fish swimming in its path. The end of the net is the cod end where about 150 pounds of fish converge. The net is pulled up every few hours on to the trawl deck, at the aft, or back of the boat. From there, the fish is dumped into a hatch to the factory below, and then sorted, processed and frozen. *Saga Sea* fished for pollock, which meant her seasons ranged from winter months in the Bering Sea and Gulf of Alaska to summer and fall in the Gulf of Alaska exclusively.

Later, as I toiled in the galley, a production line foreman said he was surprised to learn that this was my first trip. I was pleased by the compliment because I'd been working my tail off at the job and suffering the slings and arrows of Paul's criticisms. The wheelhouse would become a constant place of refuge and intrigue for me. I spent as much of my spare time as I could up there.

One night when we were out of sight of land, I went up to the wheelhouse. Gazing over the pitch-black sea into the night sky, millions of stars shone clearer and more brightly than anything I'd ever seen on land. It was as though a galaxy-filled orb had encased the *Saga Sea*, stretching from one endless end of the horizon to the other and reaching out into infinite space. It was one of the most stunning, beautiful sights I've ever seen, as well as one of the most humbling. I felt very small under that massive, brilliant, celestial sphere. I breathed that still moment in and felt at peace.

Galley crew on the *Saga Sea*.

Chief Steward John Bloomfield (RIP) on top of the tundra at Captain's Bay, Dutch Harbor, Alaska.

The view from a porthole on a beautiful day out on the sea.

John Bloomfield, my first boss, on the "veranda" of the *Saga Sea* having a smoke and coffee break.

Enjoying the view of OSI Dock Two, Captain's Bay, Unalaska.

John and Marcy enjoying happy hour.

Chief Steward John Bloomfield cleans up a stormy mess in the storeroom on the *Saga Sea*.

With Paul, the First Cook who harassed me (left); Lee MacDonald (right) and me (center) trying to peacefully navigate a difficult situation in the *Saga Sea* galley.

Learning how to make Norwegian Potato balls was a huge productionin my *Saga Sea* days. Now I can make them with my eyes closed.

Paul, the First Cook loved his knives and had numerous scars.

Early days on the *Saga Sea* - salad bar.

Mending torn fish nets on the *Saga Sea*.

180 tons of fish in the net aboard the *Saga Sea*.

Bag of Pollock on the *Saga Sea*.

Two huge bags of fish on the *Saga Sea*.

Me and birds (adult eagles/juvenile eagles).

Birds surrounding the boat, Prince William Sound.

Shark on deck of the *Saga Sea*.

Salmon spawning in Prince
William Sound.

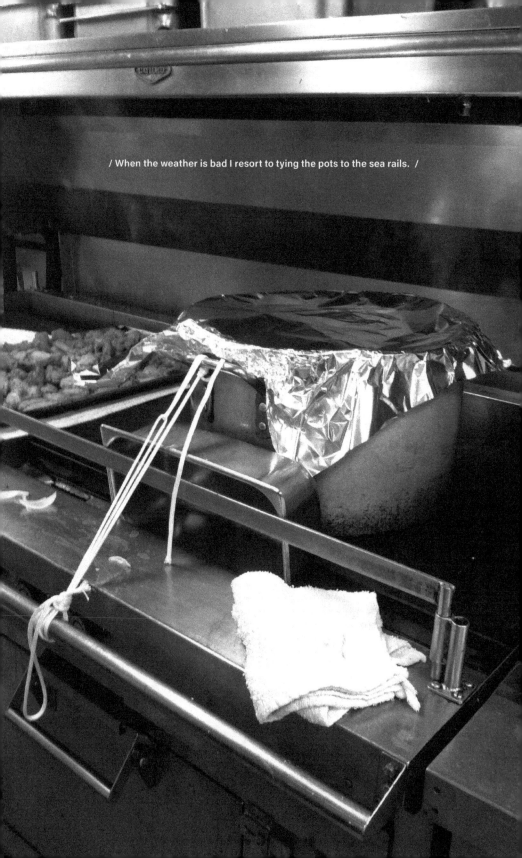

/ When the weather is bad I resort to tying the pots to the sea rails. /

Cooking in the Wind and Waves

When you're out to sea, preparing a meal is far different from being on land because in addition to all the cooking and cleaning, you need to brace yourself as the boat rocks to keep your balance. Since everything in the galley is made of metal - the countertops, sinks, ovens, and stoves – you're also continuously being thrown against hard, rough surfaces. Twice during heavy weather, while cleaning up spillage from the storm, I slipped in the galley and slammed into the corner edge of a bulkhead, hitting my leg and head, suffering whiplash in my neck.

Moving hot food from the oven or cooking with grease could be treacherous, too. I learned that firsthand when a sudden swell caused me to fall sideways while I was carrying a pan filled with chicken and hot grease. The sheet pan flipped toward me as the boat rolled, I grabbed for the counter rail to stabilize myself, and OMG! Hot oil spewed through the galley, searing my foot quite badly.

Also, boat stoves and counters are built with rails designed to keep food from sliding onto the floor, but you need to be careful because with all that pitching and rolling during a storm boiling hot water can spill over the rails. I was burned more than once.

Being in a storm at sea is like being in a washing machine on spin cycle. You're pitched forward and aft as the boat rises against the waves and slams suddenly down. To keep cakes even, I had to spin them in the oven because the cooking surface wasn't consistently level, struggling to keep my body erect in the process. This constant balancing act required tightening of my leg muscles hour after hour. Doing this type of calisthenics while juggling pots and pans filled heavy with food is challenging even for the most fit people. All that pushing, pulling, lunging, grasping, running and lifting while just trying to just stay upright is a workout. I was in good shape when I boarded the *Saga Sea*, but I certainly wasn't an athlete. It was a heart-pounding, muscle aching, relentless, non-stop fitness workout. Being at sea also amplifies the appetite, so I had to move fast to get the meals out since everyone waiting for them was more than eager to eat.

When I first started cooking on *Saga Sea*, the meals were somewhat basic – one entrée, a starch, vegetable, green salad, and dessert. Fish (pollock, salmon, halibut, shrimp or calamari) was always on the menu, as well as all kinds of potato dishes (scalloped, au gratin, smashed spuds, baked, and French fries). Spaghetti was also always a crew pleaser. I always served hamburgers on Fridays, hot dogs regularly, and my mother's famous "Peter skis," or known by their proper name, piroshkies. I suspect my mother found pronouncing piroshky difficult, so she renamed the small puff pastry filled with meat and vegetables "Peter skis." Hot out of the oven stuffed and steaming, they were delicious and happily wolfed down by crew.

Later, as I became more adventurous with my menus, I branched out to serving Asian stir fries and fried rice, pot roasts, pork chops, prime rib and other steaks, and lots of chicken. I curried chicken, fried, and baked it. I doused it in Yoshida teriyaki sauce and stuffed the flank. I also cooked turkey meals, including everything you might imagine seeing on a traditional Thanksgiving table – stuffing, cranberry sauce, peas, carrots, spiced yams, and pumpkin pie. Always intent on satisfying the tastes of everyone aboard, sometimes my ambition to please led to what was for me also very unusual cooking. The African crew aboard loved Maafe, an African peanut butter stew made with lamb, chicken, or beef with yams, hot spices, tomato paste, and peanut butter. The Filipino crew also liked cooked chicken feet with the claws removed and boiled cow feet, though I must confess, I let other cooks prepare these delicacies.

The First Cook was responsible for breakfast, a midnight meal, and all baking. Their meals usually consisted of standard breakfast bill-of-fare, such as omelets, scrambled eggs or eggs benedict, bacon or sausage.

Dinner was the toughest meal to prepare and serve, but lunch was difficult too. Deciding what to cook was sometimes even contingent on the swells. One day, the boat was rocking and rolling so dramatically, it was throwing me all around the galley. To avoid sending spaghetti or whatever I'd cooked that day for lunch or dinner into the air, I braced myself between the pots and the roll and pitch of the ocean.

Despite my best efforts to feed everyone substantial, healthy meals, numerous people inevitably got seasick, retching what little food I'd cooked that they'd managed to eat. The sight of people losing their food, particularly the inexperienced, first-time boaters, was one I would see a lot during my career.

Before going to bed that night after working all day in the galley, I was bemused to see countless "boat bruises" covering my arms, hips and shins. This would also be something I would frequently see on my body from head-to-toe. It was just part of my job. But in those early days, I was thankful to have been hired as a cook's assistant. I chopped vegetables, mixed food, washed dishes, helped plan meals, kept a record of stock and helped purchase supplies when we went ashore. It was exhausting work, but not nearly as gritty a job as being a fish processor. It was hard for me to see all the waste that went on in the factory, with so much fish thrown out. I just knew we were all going to go to hell for killing all those fish for the sake of money.

Later in my fishing career, I wanted to find out what fish processors went through by working side-by-side with them. So, I went to the factory to understand the extent of their job. I discovered processing was a horrible job, and even rougher because processers weren't always well-respected. The work was rigorous. I learned firsthand that they worked tirelessly for nearly 16 hours at a time in all phases of the process, from cutting the heads off fish, grinding pollock into paste, loading and unloading product, to putting fish into the freezer hold. It was mindless, repetitious factory-style work which had to be done rapidly. The pace was beyond exhausting, leaving them little time or energy to do anything but sleep during their time off. Plus, the engine room was swelteringly hot and loud, and this noise and heat extended across the bottom of the boat, making the factory an almost unbearably steamy place to work. If the catch was good for pollock, which it often was during the winter, they'd generally make pretty good money. With luck, some roe would be included in the catch. These tiny egg sacks could bring a hefty price. Called sujiko, they were considered a delicacy in Japan. Roe-sorting proved very profitable for them. During a successful fishing trip, the factory could be buzzing 24-hours a day to fill it to capacity within three weeks. But, if the fishing was light or even terrible, the lack of fish meant they didn't get paid anything. Sometimes we could be out to sea for nearly two months without ever seeing land, ever in search of that next big haul.

Though at the expense of others, sometimes I'd get lucky and get some help in the galley. People getting "kick shifts," or extra hours because they'd been caught in their rooms or in the dinner line before it was time for their shift to eat, were sent to the galley for a few hours.

Two weeks into my first fishing trip, my arm and hand began to bother me. Fishing is not for the weak, and to be quite honest, it's a job best suited for the young. It's physically very taxing. In my 30s, I wasn't by any stretch of the imagination old, but I wasn't a teenager either. I felt the work in my muscles a lot.

As the years went by, the crews and the menus expanded. To accommodate the different crew we had on board, I had to first take care of the Norwegians. Though it was never articulated as such, those who were smart knew the Norwegians were the crew to please first. They paid our paychecks! This is the main reason I learned very quickly to make kumla, or potato balls.

Potato balls are a Norwegian staple and with so many Norwegians aboard the *Saga Sea*, making them was necessary. Also known as potato klub, or potato dumplings, these soft, chewy bacon-infused potato balls are a sometimes called a "poor man's meal" since potatoes are plentiful and inexpensive in Norway. Smooth with a gnocci-like texture, potato balls are soaked in a base of lamb or beef stock to give them their soft consistency.

The day I first tasted potato balls, I never guessed how often I'd be making them during my career. To make them, I adapted a traditional Norwegian recipe, which to this day I share with no one. I've since become known for my special version of this tasty smoosh of potato, bacon, and flour rolled tightly into a soft ball. I've perfected my "balls" to the point of becoming very well-known for my ball-making skills! When we are docked in Seattle between seasons, I continue to cook aboard the boats. For years the Norwegians have been making the trip to Pier 90 specifically to have my balls on Thursdays. I say with no apology, based on countless feedback from the crews I served, that my potato balls are unmatched morsels of delectability. Crews never stop asking for them. I suspect they nostalgically remind the Norwegians of their moms and home. Potato balls have become my signature dish. I can now make them in my sleep. To this day, the saying goes that I make the "best balls in the fleet." Once we even held a "ball making contest" just to see if that was true. The challengers were Ove Brekke, June Hansen (Sig Hansen's wife), Roger Mjetevik (American Seafood Company's VP), and of course, me! We invited many friends from the office and other folks from the fishing industry to judge a blind tasting competition. It boiled down to tie between me and Ove, with our hosts Joe and Hanne Sweeny's three kids as the tie breakers. Well, Ove won by a very, very small margin. Ove simmers his balls in more lamb juice than I do, so I'm convinced these kids who had been raised on lamb were very familiar with the flavor of lamb, which is why he won. Okay, so this is my book and my food story, but that is how I remember it "going down!" I still, however, have not lived down the fact I lost out to Ove.

Years later as the crews became more diverse, the menus had to change. Today, we are serving two to three entrees every meal, with many different salad choices, as well as an entire buffet line. I believe American Seafood has some of the best chefs in the industry.

Ordering food has always been extremely challenging, though, and this is no different now than it was when I first began cooking. As Stewards, we must get our orders in a computer right after we leave the dock in Seattle for it to reach Dutch Harbor in time for our first offloads. We typically need to get the orders in by Monday so they can be put together on that Friday, shipped from Seattle, and delivered to Dutch Harbor in time. From start to finish, the process takes about three weeks. But I must rely on good communication from the captain needing food to determine when his boat's estimated time of arrival would be in Dutch Harbor. But if the fishing is good on the day I speak with him and I order food based on when he projects his boat might arrive in Dutch Harbor and then the fishing is bad, the boat might not arrive for a week or more after the food. Or if the fishing is exceptionally good and fast, the boat could arrive in Dutch Harbor before the food. Miscalculation can either mean that produce sits on the dock in Dutch Harbor and spoils or we miss our load altogether. Buying food in Dutch Harbor to replace a lost load is also very expensive and frowned on by the office. This unpredictability in fishing always means there is a lot to consider when I order food. There is also the added challenge of having to guess what my crew's eating habits and/or culture might be before ordering the food. It does, and did, include a lot of guess work.

Cooking sweetbread on the *Saga Sea*.

Coffee break with Roger in the *Saga Sea* dry stores.

Candy, *Saga Sea* galley assistant, came right out of high school to help on the *Saga Sea* and her dad also worked on the boat.

Cooking chicken cordon bleu on the *Saga Sea*

Cooking octopus.

Sorting lucrative fish roe.

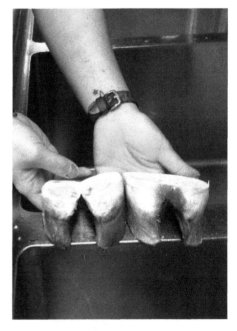

Cow feet prepared for the Filipino crew on the *Northern Hawk*.

Cooked chicken feet for the Filipino crew on the *Northern Hawk*.

Stir fry for 120 crew mates on the *Katie Ann*.

John Bloomfield, Chief Steward (RIP) simmers potato balls on the *Saga Sea*.

Saga Sea Chief Steward John Bloomfield stands in the galley of the *Saga Sea*. Listing of the vessel caused everything to tilt to one side and food to slide in that direction.

Roger teaches me to make my famous potato balls (kumla).

Pot of my famous "potato" balls!

Beef pot pie, shrimp casarole.

Learning how to fillet salmon on the *Saga Sea*.

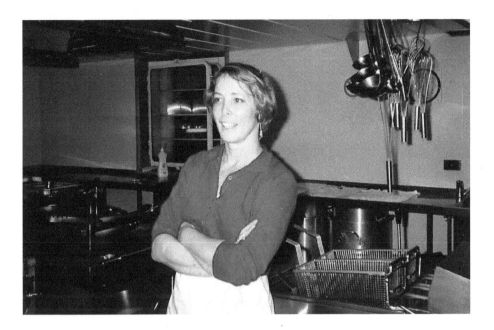

Fill-in steward on the *Saga Sea*, Bobi Berry.

John Bloomfield (RIP) has fun twirling soup ladles in the *Saga Sea* galley.

/ Young eagles often nest on the *Saga Sea* fishing nets. /

Fishing in the
Bering Sea and Alaska

We were headed for Amaknak Island in Unalaska, Alaska, located about 900 miles southwest of Anchorage. Our first docking would be in Dutch Harbor, a factory town on Amaknak Island located on an inlet of Unalaska Island, about halfway down Alaska's Aleutian Island chain. Our processor crew would be unloading pollock there. We'd have our choice of getting off the boat to go into town and making phone calls home, going to the store or post office, or grabbing a few coveted hours of uninterrupted sleep. Despite my urge to sleep instead, I would be jumping off to make a phone call. First and foremost, I wanted to find out how my dad's health was doing, not to mention talk with my daughter, Shana, and goddaughter, Jenny.

Steaming through the Aleutian Islands, my first view of Unimak Pass was nothing short of awe-inspiring. The Aleutian Islands follow the western side of the Alaskan peninsula. Pollock spawn here, making it an especially fertile fishing ground for commercial fishing vessels like the *Saga Sea*. Passes between the Aleutian Islands connect the Bering Sea to the Pacific Ocean, and Unimak Pass is no exception. Our ultimate destination would be the Bering Sea.

Turning north through the Gulf of Alaska, Unimak Pass links the Pacific Ocean to the Bering Sea. Humpback whales, sea lions, sea otters, turtles, puffins, and cormorants are often seen in this area. I was excited by the prospect of possibly seeing them. What I did see right away was the reddish peaks of stunning volcanic mountains and a bevy of migratory birds I couldn't identify. This was sight enough to thrill me. John, the Chief

Steward, and I would be going into Dutch Harbor the next day. I was more than ready to feel my "land legs."

Entering the Bering Sea, the ocean became very choppy, caused apparently by its relatively shallow water. I was concerned about John. He'd been drinking every day, and not just the boxed wine I used for cooking. I'd noticed he'd had ice cubes in his coffee one morning, and sticking my finger into it, I'd tasted strong scotch. I knew that taste. He'd asked me if I wanted to share a beer with him and when I'd said, "no," he'd retorted, "well, you're no fun." It was the first time since I'd stopped drinking that I'd considered it. I staunchly replied, "I'm lots of fun without alcohol." But I could see how sobriety could be a greater challenge than other places working on a fishing vessel. The culture almost demanded it. I could certainly see how someone might start drinking again fishing. I was amazed at how available it was, despite strict regulations against it.

In the early days of my fishing experience, drinking was customary and even expected, especially off the ship. Still relatively new to sobriety, I often met with my two friends aboard who I'd known from Alcoholic Anonymous (AA) to voice my concerns and get my bearings. Sometimes I'd listen to tapes from an AA fellowship just to hear familiar voices share their stories. It helped me feel better about staying on track with my commitment to myself.

In those early years, only officers had televisions in their rooms, and the company provided them with VHS tapes and movies. Now, everyone aboard a fishing vessel has a TV in their rooms. Times have changed a lot. But back then you were very cool if you had a television. John had one in his room, which, of course, smelled like booze. But I didn't care because he had a television, and while it was forbidden for me to be there, I would go to his room solely to watch TV.

When we arrived in Dutch Harbor in the morning. I couldn't wait to get off and find a phone. I'd been more than two weeks on the water, which at this point felt like two months. In those early days, communication was only readily available through snail mail, which could take weeks to reach the vessel. As inconceivable as it seems today with our easy access to computers and cell phones worldwide, and daily phone calls and texts being the norm, back then, phone calls from sea cost $10 a minute. So, generally you had to wait for a long time to hear anything from home, baring emergency communications. I was more than ready to call home. I ached for news about my dad. Hearing his voice for the first time in weeks was a huge relief. He seemed fine. Once I had the confidence, he was okay, I hung up the phone and took a short walk through town. The hills around me were beautiful, covered in green heather. Dirt and mud clumped under my feet. I could feel the earth rocking. When you've been out to sea for any length of time, you get "your sea legs." Your equilibrium is rearranged. Then, when you get off the boat, you can barely stand up because the land feels like it's moving side to side. Unsteady, I wobbled my way back to the boat. That night, we headed off to the fishing grounds in the Bering Sea, about fourteen hours away. Now *Saga Sea* would show us if she could truly catch fish and start making all of us real money.

The following morning, we shot a net for the first time and pulled up about six tons of Pollock. Since *Saga Sea*'s equipment had never been used, the factory crew had their hands full adjusting the necessary machinery for more fish. A haul is usually 70 tons of fish and doesn't take long to run through processing. The nets can hold up to 150 tons of fish. But we had a leak in the engine room and crew broke a bolt while trying to fix it. Suddenly we were dead in the water, something that would happen a lot in my fishing career. While we waited for a couple of hours, John said he thought that I could work my way up to First Cook in no time at all. I felt very complimented, but I also knew I was working hard. It felt good to be recognized for my efforts.

Despite valiant effort, our first few hauls were small at 50 tons, but on our third haul, a whopping 150 tons came up. That's when I had my first view of how huge a commercial haul of fish can be. During all that excitement, the boat was rocking a lot against 10-foot swells. Crew had forgotten to switch the fuel over to adjust our load, so we were riding at a five-degree list in the morning. Fish water and fuel leaked into our fresh water supply, which is why to this day I don't drink boat water of any kind. Power went out completely and we had trouble with the engine. For days, we continued to have problems with daily blackouts and toilets backing up, including mine. To use the bathroom, I'd have to trot up two flights of stairs to the wheelhouse.

On her first trip, the *Saga Sea* had numerous startup problems. We weathered them together. Making good of uncomfortable situations, every night when I'd go up to the wheelhouse, I'd stay for a while and chat with Captain Kurt. It was peaceful up there. I was fascinated by the computerized Bridge, the ship's command room. From his computer, Captain Kurt could see schools of fish and the net activity electronically. The fish didn't have a chance. We had an easy, comfortable friendship. He'd tease me, saying I always went to bed too early and missed the wheelhouse parties.

On August 15, 1990, I celebrated my upcoming birthday and three other crew mates' birthdays. Drinking was not an option for me, but that day I was sorely tempted. The day my contract was up, October 11, 1990, seemed insurmountably far away. My adventure was losing its shine behind sewage clogged toilets, cracked fish holding tanks, sprained ankles, and squished hands. Fifteen-foot swells rocked the boat. I felt homesick and missed my daughter. I tried not to think about her, but love overtook me. I missed her so much. When they lowered the skiff to jet over and pick up new crew, I very nearly asked to leave. Three people had already quit, but two came back. In approximately eight more days, we'd be back at Dutch Harbor to repair the boat. I decided to hold on but had to swallow my disappointment when I learned the *Claymore Sea*, one of our sister ships, would be going into Dutch Harbor ahead of us. Our Chief Engineer had hurt his ankle and needed to be air-lifted off the boat and we couldn't proceed without getting another engineer with papers to prove he'd had at least six months of service in charge of an engine-room watch on fishing vessels. Our docking would be delayed by two weeks.

Thinking I might like to work as a BAADER driver during the delay, I went down to the factory. To help during roe season, some of us would help the processing crew pull roe for two to three hours after having already worked 12 to 14-hour shifts of our own. The process of preparing fish for our customers was quite detailed, as well as heavily regulated. Sorters pulled fish off the decks into large bins and sorted them for size. Then it was weighed electronically. I became enthralled by the BAADER driver, a machine that beheads, cuts, and filets fish at 123 fish per minute. There was something exhilarating about watching the machine's precision in action as it rolled the fish on a conveyer belt and then dropped onto a transfer belt. Paddles scooped out its innards, it was fileted and skinned, and then dropped down again to a candling table where the fish was backlit to check for parasites. The fish was then cleaned, deboned and sent to packers, where it was compressed into boxes and frozen in plate freezers for two hours. It was then dropped below through a chute to crew known as "freezer rats" who stacked the boxes in the boat's freezer hold. The hold was the impressive length of a football field. Everything that was not fileted, boxed, and frozen was ground into a fine powder and sold primarily to Japan as food for eels and as fertilizer. Today, every piece of the fish is accounted for and used. The final disbursement is weighed to be certain it matches the weight of the original haul.

In the years I served on factory fishing vessels, to know what my crewmates were experiencing, I ended up learning every job involved in fish production. It is grueling, repetitious, slimy work. I am ever impressed with the grit fishing factory workers display daily. Fishing is also vital to employment in the Greater Seattle area. With many of Seattle's natural resource industries gone, such as sawmills, milled wheat and canned produce companies, fishing has endured amidst its famed coffee culture, software, computer, and biotech industries, retail giants, and global trade and aerospace industries. But, even with this precision, the efficient use of every part of what we caught and its vitality to my hometown's economy, I couldn't help but have the unsettling feeling that we were raping the sea dry. Our nets were huge. To give you an idea of their size, in the Pacific Northwest our Tacoma Dome sports arena is 530 feet (160 m) in diameter and 152 feet (46 m) tall. Our fishing nets, when underway and fully spread, were the same size. Trawling hundreds of miles, we caught everything within that radius. Due to fishing regulation, we were only allowed to fish for pollock, but other fish were caught in the net, such as cod, crab, and halibut. We had no license to fish for these, so it was illegal to keep them. We had to throw back anything that wasn't pollock or hake. The discarded fish often perished in the process, a fact that always bothered me. There was so much unnecessary waste. The Halibut Commission was extremely strict, though. However, despite this environmental concern, our large freezer-trawler could fish further away from continental shelves and more vulnerable marine habitats than smaller fishing boats, so it was a trade-off. Our technology was also very advanced. The huge wheelhouse of the *Saga Sea* had so many satellite tracking, monitoring, and data collection computers, it looked like a commercial film editing studio. Technological improvements are made to this day to reduce unnecessary catch, and of course, protect the lives of those aboard. Today's vessels have cameras attached to the nets to show exactly what fish are going into the nets. It's quite amazing.

Sometimes, though, regardless of the Halibut Commissioner's edicts, we would keep the fish and cook it. It was common knowledge that no one on any of the fishing vessels obeyed the law. Like drinking, the officers did it anyway, despite the rules. The Norwegians built a state of art "still" on the *Saga Sea* until the office found it and they had to remove it. Since *Saga Sea* was a boat that had come to the U.S. from Norway, her Fish Master, Arild, was Norwegian. In truth, he was the "head honcho" aboard. Due to maritime law, however, he wasn't allowed to drive the vessel in American waters. So, when Captain Kurt was sleeping, an American First Mate always had to be in the wheelhouse. During these times, crab and cocktails were a common occurrence in Arild's room. The Government Observer aboard was also paid to make sure everything was compliant. However, she was easily distracted from not reporting everything. She was young and this was her first contract. Who would check them miles out to sea, if not the Government Observer? A lot must have not been reported because our Observer would later become Captain Kurt's wife. We became a quirky type of family so many miles from land, no matter what our given positions.

The night before had been rocky. I'd had difficulty sleeping. I worked nights, so my biological clock was turned around. Tossing on the waves hadn't helped my insomnia, either. Often after hours of working in the galley, the combination of tired muscles and working at a fast pace left me restless when I tried to sleep. Looking out my porthole window, the fog had been deep and thick. I hadn't been able to see anything through the muck. On these nights blanketed in fog, I couldn't help but nervously hope Captain Kurt was alert.

On Tuesday, August 28, 1990, we steamed into Dutch Harbor. We'd picked up a few people who'd had injuries or wanted to quit from two other boats, the *Heather Sea* and *Claymore Sea*. The next day, it was discovered one of the young women who was berthed in my room had been "hot bunking" with one of the guys on board. "Boat hoes" were notorious for shamelessly bedding all the male crew. There was always promiscuity aboard. On this occasion, both the young woman and her male partner got head lice. At first, they said it was crabs, but on closer inspection, it was head lice. So, I was quarantined to my room alongside my three other crew mates. I was also subjected to a very demoralizing, scary experience. The housekeeper inspected my privates with a magnifying glass. I was so mad at my crew mate, I started crying. Luckily, my internment wasn't long. Captain Kurt also said he planned to get me a better room. Being friends with the wheelhouse crew guaranteed perks like these.

When reviewed, we learned *Saga Sea* had hauled over 112 tons of fish in her maiden voyage, more than any boat had ever done on its first trip. To celebrate this victory, John and I went to the Uni-Sea Bar. Our Observer, Arild, and Captain Kurt met us there. I drank water all night while our observer, the captain, and Arild got "three-sheets-to-the wind" drunk. The observer could have very well lost her job by drinking and hobnobbing with the crew. But by the end of the night, she had lost all inclination to report anything. She and Captain Kurt were cuddled up closely and fooling around. It turns out they weren't the only people breaking the rules that night. Returning to the boat, we discovered our bosun, Rick and our purser, Marcy, had taken a skiff out after dark, which was against all laws in those waters. We'd run all over the boat looking for them and they hadn't been anywhere. Being very careful not to alarm the rest of our crew, I took our observer up to the wheelhouse to stay with the Captain. He called the Coast Guard and police, who did an extensive search of the water, to no avail. Rick and Marcy finally returned to the boat around 3:30 A.M. and ended up in bed together, where Phyllis and Arild finally found them. The incident, however, was kept quiet. Rick and Marcy were favored by those who would have reported them.

It had been over a month since I'd been to an AA meeting. Since I had credit for a free taxi ride, I decided to go to a meeting while the boat was in port for repairs. Charlie, my boyfriend from home, had a boat repair shop in Dutch Harbor, so I was looking forward to seeing him. Once in town, Lisa and I met John at the UniSea Bar. He was sitting next to a guy who kept looking hard at me. Finally, the guy asked, "Are you Sindi Haglund?" To my surprise, I realized it was Ronnie Ziegler (RIP). We'd grown up in the same neighborhood. It was fun to see a familiar face. Ron was well known in Dutch Harbor.

Crew often went into town making up for lost time by getting drunk, but while in Dutch Harbor, John and I took a hike up a mountain covered in blueberry bushes and picked blueberries. It was like walking on a plush carpet. On the way down, John fell into a hole up to his waist. He wasn't hurt, but the look on his face was one of such complete surprise, I laughed so hard, I started to cry. Later that week, Marcy, the observer, and I had a party in John's room. They had rum and coke and I had coke, but I was the one who ended up with a lampshade on my head! Marcy spilled a drink on my head and then knocked the lampshade off. It landed perfectly upright on my head. It was hilarious. I cherish the memory of our times together. We were the best of friends. I was also not looking forward to working in the galley without John and reporting to Paul.

Being in port was a mixed blessing. On the one hand, I was able to get off the boat and feel land under my feet, which was my favorite part of fishing. But it also meant I had to feed as many as 50 extra people, which was exhausting. I'd finished my first fishing adventure and already felt myself wishing I could get out to sea again. Two days later, on that Thursday, I got my wish. After the last line was untied, we left Dutch Harbor. The Norwegians were superstitious about leaving port on a Friday, which was no doubt a carry-over from days of old when Friday was said to be an unlucky day because it was the day Christ was crucified. Luckily, the superstition of having a seafaring woman aboard was no longer applicable. Legend claimed that having a woman aboard caused friction among sailors, distracting them and making the sea angry. My experience with Paul certainly upheld that notion of friction. But, in the day of old, the term "son of a gun" also came from sailors who consummated their affairs on the gun deck before arriving in port. Naked women were said to have a calming effect on the sea, which is why the figureheads on old ships are of naked women. We had our "boat hoes," so our crew had their fair share of naked women to appease the wild seas.

Unalaska.

Looking out at the bay, Dutch Harbor, Alaska.

In the Bering Sea, the Coast Guard would do random boardings of our boats to check what we were doing. They were constantly watching us to be sure we were compliant with fishing regulations.

Fishing in the Bering Sea, Alaska; Arild, Fish master, and Adres, Foreman.

With John Bloomfield in the *Saga Sea* galley. He looks sad because he had just learned that I was leaving the *Saga Sea*.

Lee, a drunk crew member, and my son, Chuck, trying to contain her.

Wally Chipock (RIP), Foreman on the *Saga Sea*. He was a good friend and boat mate. I miss him.

Two bags of fish, probably 130 to 150 tons each, on the *Saga Sea* split trawl deck.

On the *Saga Sea*, our nets accidentally caught a walrus. It was deceased by the time we pulled it in. One of our crewmates wanted its tusks, so he beheaded it and threw it back into the water headless. Our nets then caught it again and dredged it back aboard. Those monitoring our catch were surprised at the headless walrus.

Driving around Unalaska.

Welcome to OSI Bunkhouse, a bunkhouse for crews awaiting their boats. A real "rat hole."

Orthodox Russian Church with an interesting history in Unalaska.

A very old cemetery next to the church.   The view from across the bay to Unalaska.

We often saw eagles. Stately and enormous, these birds were quite impressive.

With a crewmate in front of the same Orthodox Russian Church in Unalaska after a fresh dusting of snow.

/ We also weathered the days on the *Saga Sea* by goofing around! Here, Rick Meyers frames my face with the teeth he extracted from a shark. /

Weathering the Days

Thankfully, it wasn't all work on the *Saga Sea*. For as much work as the galley was, we also had a lot of fun. And when we played, we played hard, fast, and lively. To ease the tension of lack of sleep and storms, there were often playful, asexual moments aboard. Weeks on end aboard a fishing vessel can build a kind of bottled stress unlike anything you'd experience on land. The combination of exhaustion and loneliness can make even the most stalwart personality wither. So, we had to do something to break the monotony and angst aboard, and that something became food fights. On my first couple of fishing trips, these were very much the norm. A parcel of grown adults packed into that pressure-cooker of a galley became a bunch of unleashed, rambunctious kids. During one such food fight, I was transformed into a Mount McKinley of whipped cream, slathered from head to foot in a soft, sugary, fluffy mess, laughing as I squirted John with the same. We were so slathered by the end of it, we both had to take showers before going back to work. Another time, I flung a strawberry at John in the galley and it crossed his forehead and splattered on the wall. He then grabbed me and smeared a strawberry on my face, to which I retaliated by smearing one on his face. We had a lot of rollicking good times in the galley. John said I was the best Galley Assistant he'd ever had. He told me he wanted me to come back and be on his rotation and train to be a First Cook. I was quite honored. We were both Virgos and worked well together.

One day, bosun Rick was using a fire hose to wash unwanted fish off the end of the boat. The observer and I were up in the wheelhouse watching a sea lion following the boat. We were so excited, we ran down to the stern, or back end of the boat, to take photos. Halfway down the trawl deck, we heard the captain yell, "Get 'em, Rick!" We heard Rick laugh as he nailed us with a blast of water from the hose. We were soaked but laughing too.

Another time, John made me a fruit hat. I looked hilariously like Carmen Miranda, that "Brazilian Bombshell" who was made famous by wearing a hat made of fruit in her American films. One night, we pulled up a whale's head bone in our net. Captain Kurt said he planned to take it home as a souvenir of our time together. Also, we put a dead pollock in the in the First Cook's dishwater.

Another time, John made me a fruit hat. I looked hilariously like Carmen Miranda, that "Brazilian Bombshell" who was made famous by wearing a hat made of fruit in her American films.

Still another time, we grabbed a seagull off the deck. Thousands of them used to circle the boat hoping to sneak some of the day's yield. Once they landed, however, the deck was so mucky, they'd often get stuck. We would then lift them up and throw them back into flight. But this time, we decided to have a little fun with of them. I'm guessing the seagull was not amused by our frivolity, but we'd been out to sea for a long time and were sorely lacking in entertainment. So, we decided to color the seagull like a parrot with food coloring. Of course, the seagull's natural oils gave its wings a protective coating, so the food coloring did not absorb into the bird's feathers. Instead, it merely floated on its wings and underbelly. As we continued to pour more food coloring on the bird, it began squawking wildly and suddenly wrestled free of our hold. Like a masterful post-impressionist Picasso, it flapped down the trawl deck, brushing its wings like paint brushes against everything it touched, causing a rainbow of color to sweep across the boat. When we finally caught up to it, roaring with laughter, the entire trawl deck was covered in food coloring. Admitting defeat in our endeavor, we rinsed the bird and set it free. It gratefully flew away, no doubt wondering what on earth those silly humans had been doing and why they had chosen to do it to him.

When we celebrated my birthday on September 8, 1990, I cooked potatoes in a light beef broth with bacon and gravy, carrots, sausage and pork salt. Crew wished me a happy birthday and gave me cards. John gave me a present of five candy bars.

So, I have many memories of drudgery and danger, but these are always interspersed with the joy of comradery with my crew mates and memories of very happy times. It's hard to put into words how close you get with other people on a fishing vessel. Nothing is more bonding.

Mid-September that year, the fishing was slow, so crew had a small break while we spent 12-hours to find the fish. With only five days left until we reached port, we finally found 130 tons of fish. The sun broke, too, and the weather was terrific. John nursed a hangover while I soaked in the warmth. The sunset was gorgeous too, with red streaked, golden orange hues reaching across the spans of sea. Then, our luck turned so bad, there was talk of returning to Seattle in November. Our nets were getting snagged and ripping and we were pulling up nothing but mud. It was very disheartening. We'd be pulling into port soon, and as excited I was about that, I was also feeling down because John would be leaving. He'd been my best friend aboard and I'd loved working with him. I'd miss his company.

When we arrived in Dutch Harbor, we were tied up to two "trampers," boats that had no fixed port-of-call, to offload. So, we couldn't go ashore right away. But Charlie, my boyfriend from home, came aboard and was given permission to stay overnight in my room. Lorena, my roommate, was very cool about it. Charlie hung out all day on the boat with me, going briefly back into town. He returned with a book and carton of cigarettes, two highly desirable staples to me back then, before I'd quit smoking.

Once I was able to leave the boat, Charlie took me for a drive to his place. Eighteen days later when I'd completed my first contract, he was still in Dutch Harbor. Before I flew out, I stayed with him for a few days. He took me all over the island, and to the famous Elbow Room, a place that during the late 1970s and early 1980s was notoriously high-rolling, wild, and known for being the rowdiest bar in the U.S. But, by now, it had calmed down a bit. We ran into Rick Johnson, a guy I'd known from Ballard. That far from home, it was curious to see two people I knew from home. It felt great to see familiar faces in that stark, windswept harbor.

Relaxing on "the veranda" of the *Saga Sea*.

We became like family on the *Saga Sea*. I am seen here with Borgeir (RIP), the BAADER Tech and Lorena, the housekeeper.

Lisa, the Observer and Rick Meyers, the Bosun, playing with crab on the deck.

During my first contract, my boyfriend at the time, Chuck Miller, (pictured on the right) was stationed at Dutch Harbor. It was comforting to have him there.

Nancy (RIP), a quality control manager, decided to have some fun with a seagull and doused it with food coloring. The result was the seagull created an abstract painting on the deck as it flapped around on it.

Lee MacDonald is doused in whipped cream during a food fight on the *Saga Sea*.

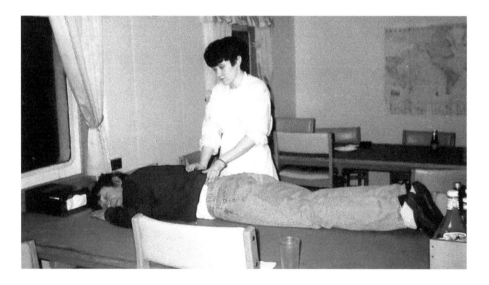

My daughter, Shana, going the extra mile for crewmates on the *Saga Sea*. This would never happen in today's world!

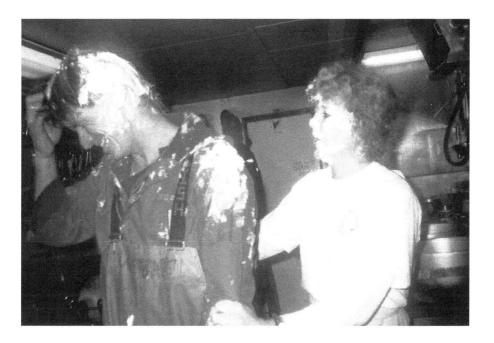

This is how we relaxed on the *Saga Sea*; Joe Westgate and me.

Food fights released stress, Val QC (RIP) Phyllis' housekeeper; Mike; first cook Donna, Russian Galley Assistant.

/ Out on the rough seas. /

Navigating the Angry Seas

When the swells move underwater rather than chopping on the surface, it's a sure sign a storm is ahead. Birds can also be seen flying low and heading to shore to take refuge if bad weather is on the way. But unlike savvy birds, in late September 1990, *Saga Sea* was heading full steam into a storm. Since our stern ramp hadn't been fixed properly yet, I was praying it wouldn't split. Looking out my porthole, I could see distant lights from other ships surfacing on the horizon, and then dipping out of sight under the heavy swells. The boat was leaping under me. Sometimes far out to sea, the winds could blow as fiercely as 90-miles an hour, causing massive, jarring swells. There's nothing quite like the heart-in-your throat exhilaration, bordering on fear, that you get as you're thrown around during one of these mammoth storms.

Despite the wild seas, our fishing had been good. Breaking over 100 tons of frozen product was a record for the *Saga Sea* and doing it during a storm even more so. By this time, we were hauling in tons of fish and funneling them into our below-deck freezer hold, which meant we'd likely have a shorter trip. Every day was netting 90 to 120 tons of fish.

I'd already been anticipating port and we'd only been fishing for five days. Captain Frank, who was the captain aboard the *Saga Sea* during my second contract, said if we continued to fish as we had been, we'd be full in ten days. This was of some comfort since the weather was so wild. Gale force winds of up to 40 miles an hour hit the boat, making even standing difficult, let alone work in the galley. This storm would prove mild compared to others we would later face. I wasn't sleeping well due to all the rocking and was coming down with a cold.

Captain Frank didn't seem to be as social as Captain Kurt had been, so I'd wait until Arild was in the wheelhouse to go up there. An unassuming, slight man with a quiet presence, though not intimidating, Captain Frank was a man of few words. However, when he talked about fishing, his serious brown eyes would instantly light up. Deeply committed to his job, I would learn later that he came from a long line of fisherman and loved fishing. His father had been raised in Costa Rica and had fished for shrimp. Following migratory tuna to San Diego, California, his dad had met and married his mom. Captain Frank had been raised in the family fishing tradition in San Diego. By the time he was twenty-two years old, he'd already crewed on whale watching boats and fished for tuna in the Eastern and Western Pacific, Africa, and New Zealand. Captain Frank became the first non-Norwegian Captain to ever take the helm of the *Saga Sea*. In later years, he would make a professional career in the fishing industry, taking lead roles in company operations and compliance. But he would look back on our *Saga Sea* years with nostalgia due to the fact that laws in the workplace aboard the ship were relatively non-restrictive at that time. Disagreements were negotiated on the spot and settled in real time, face-to-face. In contrast, grievances on fishing trawlers today are entered by the complainant on a computer, routed to the central office on land, sent back to the boat, and settled through a stream of paperwork and documentation. Settling an issue can take an inordinate amount of time and be very costly.

Though I had a few times when I felt highly harassed in my fishing career, I never felt my work wasn't valued as much as any man on board. The nature of the work we were doing demanded respect, regardless of gender. Once I climbed that gangplank and set my feet on the deck, I became crew, independent of being a woman. Captain Frank would later say that the women aboard often worked harder and more efficiently than the men, perhaps because we were staunchly trying to make sure we carried our weight. We were serious about proving ourselves. I, for one, was unshakeable in my resolve to succeed.

On the morning of my second contract, we had a Captain's meeting and safety drill, as we always did on the first day of a new trip. Mark, the first mate, couldn't inspire anyone to put on a survival suit, so he randomly asked which life raft was assigned to each person. When he came to me, I answered, and to my surprise, he said I was wrong. So, I demonstrated how to put the bulky, oversized, bright orange survival suit on in less than one minute. Everyone said they'd never seen it done so well. Later I found out I'd been right about which raft was mine, which gave everyone a good laugh, including me. But, the seriousness of survival suits is no laughing matter. If you fall in the frigid water without one, you can be dead in mere minutes. With one, you can survive for up to six hours. They're designed to protect you against hypothermia.

We'd only been out to sea a little over a week and our fish freezer hold was nearly half-full. It felt good to be making money. I was also hopeful my situation with Paul would change when we had a food fight and he began to call me "Princess." Lee, our 2nd Cook, dubbed me "BABS (Badass Bitch Society)," a nickname that would stay with me my entire career. Months later, John would go into town and a waitress' name tag would read "BABS." John would pay her $20 for that tiny plastic badge. For years after, I wore it proudly. A group of us also laughingly called ourselves "The Surimi Weenie Club." We'd entertain ourselves by sucking Jell-O and blowing cigarette ashes on each other. This was before Jell-O shots were even invented. We had a great time laughing and telling jokes around mealtime. By the end of September, I'd also befriended Adreas, a Norwegian Factory Superintendent. Though we were never involved, I became known as his "boat girlfriend" since I took ice cream to him in the officers' mess hall every night.

In early October 1990, the fog moved in, the weather was awful, the seas were rough, and we were surrounded by seventeen other boats, all with the same mission of finding fish. Having finally met our yield, we slowly headed down south at full steam, heading to the beach. I was bone tired. My new head cook, Bobbi, was a hardcore know-it-all and driving me crazy. I was glad the second leg of my fishing adventure was nearly over.

On Christmas Day, 1990, at 3:00 A.M. after a wonderful visit home, I climbed again on a plane headed to Anchorage, Alaska. My ultimate destination was Dutch Harbor and the *Saga Sea*. The plane was filled with people from my company returning to fish. Chuck and Phyllis, from the *Claymore Sea*, were among them. I was thrilled to see Captain Kurt and John back on board.

Leaving port two days later, the seas were very rough, with 60-mile-an-hour winds. A lot of people were sick, but others weren't too sick to party. That first night was very festive. Since the party was in John's room, he got very drunk. Weary of the drinking around me, I went up to the wheelhouse for some serenity. That's where I met our new first mate, Bob, who would become a close friend of mine, and is to this day.

Work on a fishing vessel was treacherous. In late September, our First Bosun, Rick, had a huge crane hook hit his back. Two weeks later, he was in such dire pain, he went to see the doctor. Allegedly, he had a broken back, although this would prove later to be untrue. That same week, one of our new crew mates was on the deck outside the galley while the boom wench was running. It swung and hit him, breaking his arm and leg, and injuring his back and face. One of the young women aboard got hysterical when she saw his battered face, but Phyllis and I immediately leaped in to help. We rolled this guy onto the gurney and sent him by skiff back to the dock. They put him on a plane to Anchorage, coherent but in shock. We heard later he survived.

But some people were not so fortunate. On December 28, 1990, a medical emergency that haunts me to this day happened in the *Saga Sea* factory. By this time, my stepson, Chuck, was aboard working in fish processing. That day, Chuck raced into the galley, hollering, "Get up to the Bridge and find the First Mate now!" Phyllis and I called Captain Kurt, who was by then back as the Captain aboard, and woke him. As the story goes, an unfortunate crew mate, John, had been cleaning the live tanks and while lying on his back, had slipped into the tank up to his chest. The hatch's hydraulic sensor had come down on him. He had tried to slide out from under it, but it came down again, that time on his neck. After much confusion, the crew was able to extract him. Every crew member that knew CPR worked non-stop on him. A Coast Guard helicopter was about 2 ½ miles away, so we turned *Saga Sea* in its direction. About five hours after the accident, the chopper arrived, lowering a doctor to the boat's bow. The helicopter had been delayed due to fog and having had to get enough fuel in Dutch Harbor for the airlift. John's color was good from all that CPR, so we had hope. The doctor decided to stay aboard to try to save John's life. Pulling the hatch off the Trawl deck to get John out, they carried him through the galley deck, stopping every few steps to administer more CPR. He was air-lifted to a hospital in Anchorage, but everyone thought he'd been clinically dead by the time they lifted him off the boat, shortly after the accident.

The following morning our worst fears were confirmed. He had died from a crushed thorax and severed nerve that controlled breathing. If he'd survived, he'd have had to live the rest of his life on a respirator. The crew took it very hard, particularly those involved. Captain Kurt didn't sleep at all for three days. Due to a death aboard, we were required to return to port for an investigation of the accident.

Since the work we were doing was highly dangerous, casualties did happen. A sad residual from these fatal accidents was crew depression, and Chuck was in the throes of it. Since Chuck was one of the witnesses, he was among those who had to talk to the lawyers, investigators, and Coast Guard via satellite communications (Satcom). He was very shaken. He'd watched how John had been cleaning the tank and was about to do that himself but had decided he wouldn't fit in the hatch hole, so he'd climbed up and over it. He realized, with horror, that it could have easily happened to him. Later while cleaning up IVs and towels at the scene of the accident, he tried to replay what had happened. He needed to find solace in knowing it wasn't his fault. My roommate worked nights, so Chuck slept in my stateroom for days after the accident, physically sick for three days after it. Dark rumors had circulated throughout the ship that suggested Chuck might have accidentally hit the door's valve as he crawled over the tank. This thought plagued him. Even though crawling over the tank was proper protocol and he'd done what he'd been instructed to do under those circumstances, plus the fact that the hydraulics should never have been on in the first place, it still haunted him to think he might have had anything to do with John's death. The rumors and knowledge that others were suspicious of the circumstances dug his angst deeper. Val, of Quality Control, had asked Chuck if maybe he caught his sleeve on the valve, but then decided that would not have been possible. After analysis of the event, it was determined Chuck hadn't had anything to do with it. Apparently, someone who never confessed had turned the hydraulics back on which caused the sensors to work. Though investigators eventually did come on board as part of an inquiry into what happened, no one ever came forward to confess to the tragic mistake.

Death at sea is taken quite seriously by the Coast Guard. Sometimes during an investigation, they will seize a ship and keep everyone on board for up to a month. That amount of time is crucial to a fishing vessel and can wipe out a company's profits. Because the accident might have been prevented, Captain Kurt could have lost his license. Someone had flipped a wrong switch and shut the hydraulic system down. Crew hadn't been adequately trained in the hazards of working in the factory. We were instructed not to talk about the incident to anyone. The press was hungry to spin a story. Port time would be very guarded, with no one allowed off the boat.

Though our routine returned to normal the following day, the emotional impact of John's death had hit Chuck hard. Despite Chuck's foreman and Quality Control Manager telling me Chuck's work was excellent, Chuck had become violently sick and his hands had swelled. He was miserable. He told me he didn't think he was going to survive on the *Saga Sea*. The poor kid was completely traumatized. The death shook us all to the quick, but time didn't stop for Chuck or for the rest of crew. We were in full production and the fishing had to go on. Thankfully, in today's fishing world, this tragedy could never happen. Safety procedures around all equipment is now highly regulated. By the following year in January of 1991, crew had stopped talking about the death aboard.

Huge waves coming up the stern ramp. Deckhands not paying attention can get washed overboard.

Morten doing the net reel thing!

A sad day. A doctor is lowered by helicopter onto the Saga Sea to assist our crewmate, John, who had been crushed by a hatch's hydraulic sensor. The doctor pronounced John dead.

/ Up in the ice, 1997 - 1998. /

Living through Frigid Winters

As New Year's Eve, 1990 approached, John decided I should try to eat roe. So, we boiled bags of it in salted water. The roe we harvested was clustered eggs in the ovaries from female fish. Though its squishy consistency resembled cream of wheat cereal and it didn't taste too awful, just thinking about what it was, I nearly gagged trying to gulp it down. By the end of the day's work, I was so exhausted, I found myself wishing we wouldn't be partying for New Year's Eve. My feet were aching, the roe was rumbling in my stomach, and all I wanted to do was sleep into the new year. But, eating it convinced me I wanted to learn more about its production.

Even though I knew it was dangerous, that night I decided to learn even more about working in the factory in my off time, particularly about the roe line. I felt it would raise the morale of the crew to see me down there. We were towing in over one hundred tons in each haul back. When the tons were loaded with female fish, this meant we pulled in more roe. John told me on one trip that roe was worth $5,200 per share, which would have represented $10,400 per month in my pocket alone, making learning about the process intriguing and motivating.

On New Year's Eve, we were again steaming back toward Dutch Harbor to fish in the Unimak Pass area called "The Horseshoe." Though Dutch Harbor is located within the Aleutian Islands of Alaska on Amaknak Island in the Fox Islands, there's sparse little there. Its main appeal is it's a sheltered port on the Bering Sea and close to fertile fishing, although winds can get very high. It's also ice-free. History buffs are drawn to it because it was an outpost for the U.S. Army and Navy during WWII. During the 1940s,

Dutch Harbor's one bar, "Blackie's" offered cheap beer and whiskey, but no chairs because "they splintered too much in fights." Today the town has two bars that uphold its rowdy traditions. A sign hangs in front of one of them, reading, "Where fish and drink become one." In other words, enter this bar in Dutch Harbor and don't expect to leave sober. Fish to drink, and drink to fish. The two become one goal. Getting hammered was the norm and even expectation. Not surprisingly, no one recollects that I never drank anything but water in Dutch Harbor. By the end of the evening, I'm guessing no one remembered much of anything. Drinking was a stress relief for the crew, and one they relished greatly on land since, technically, they were not allowed to drink at sea. I partied with the best of them but never got hammered.

In early 1942, twenty Japanese planes bombed Dutch Harbor, but the area was rebuilt. By 1943, over ten thousand sailors were stationed at the base. However, in 1947, the base was decommissioned, leaving behind a remote, bleak harbor. Today, friends back home express interest in visiting Dutch Harbor, but it has never seemed like an appealing tourist destination to me. Its recent claim to fame and why visitors are starting to take interest in it is because since 2005 it's been featured on the Discovery Channel's reality television series, Deadliest Catch. My friend, Sig Hansen, is a featured captain on this top-rated show. Millions are glued each week to their television to watch bleary-eyed fisherman and craggy captains risk their life for a ubiquitous crab haul. While working and being filmed, crew members' fingers are smashed or sliced, or their bones get broken. Sometimes men even go overboard. In the first season of The Deadliest Catch, viewers watched transfixed as one of the featured boats sank, drowning all but one of the boat's crew. Ratings soared. Like watching gladiators fight in ancient Rome, America's television audience is riveted by the show. For me, watching the show is a harsh and poignant reminder of what it was like to live on those high seas and fight to stay alive and work in those wild winds. It truly wasn't for those without sturdy, vigorous spirits.

New Year's Eve 1990, the crew had time off, but this meant more work for me. After feeding everyone, I went up to Arild's stateroom with the Chief Steward, John, and Nancy, a Quality Control manager, to cheer, hug, and kiss in the new year. It was Nancy who would first suggest I write a book about my fishing experiences. I wrote copious journals aboard and she'd noticed me scrawling them daily into spiral notebooks. Though she has passed away, her spirit lives on in this book. A host of people attended the party that night, including our Factory Superintendent, Adreas; Engineer, Oula; Quality Control Manager, Benta; Housekeeper, Phyllis; First Boson, Gunner; and First Mate, Bob. While making our respective resolutions, champagne, whiskey and Norwegian specialty alcohols were consumed by the gallon. Though completely sober, I still dragged back to my bunk at 1:00 am, exhausted.

The next morning, I woke up, still bleary-eyed with exhaustion, to see Chuck sleeping in my roommate, Kerry's, bunk. She worked nights, so she hadn't needed it. The crew was off all day, so when Kerry came back, Chuck moved from her bunk into mine, where he slept for the rest of the day. Emotional and physical exhaustion had caught up with him, so he'd been spending a lot of time sleeping in my room when there was an empty bunk. Kerry and I decided Chuck could move in with us, at least until the end of the trip. He'd been living in an 18-man room and needed the break. That night, I'd planned to go to bed early, but Bob, the 1st Mate, and I sat in the galley and shared life stories instead. I felt trusted because he shared a lot of "boat business" with me about how everyone thinks they know better than anyone else how to run a factory boat. I hadn't known about the infighting that can happen out to sea. This same chain of conflicting communication is how rumors get started and passed around like wildfires on a boat. I was relieved when I learned that our purser, Bob, planned to pull some strings and move Chuck into a four-man room. Chuck had also mentioned interest in working topside as a deck hand. It's every bit as dangerous, if not more so, than working in the factory. But it's more money and he'd be guaranteed a better room. He was good friends with a deck hand, so that guy was going to put in a good word for him. I learned early in the close-quartered factory fishing boat environment that who you know carries a lot of weight. First and foremost, Chuck needed a long-term, quieter space. His hand had become more swollen with tendinitis. Getting his socks on had become a struggle. I was worried about him. As we approached Dutch Harbor, I also had another concern. My feet were still aching badly. I began to think about how I was going to replace my shoes with more comfortable ones.

Nearing Dutch Harbor, while anticipating the view of barren hills and barrack-like grey buildings rising in the distance, we saw something else we hadn't expected. Churning across the water, the Coast Guard was headed straight for us. We realized in short order that they would be boarding our boat soon to check our roe percentages. Most of the officers' rooms hadn't been cleaned after New Year's Eve, with empty beer, whiskey, and other alcohol bottles strewn everywhere. What a scramble! Officers raced to hide all the alcohol aboard, tossing it in the laundry room. Somehow, we cleared away the contraband in time. The Coast Guard opened and inspected nearly 30 cases of product and weighed it to be certain we weren't cheating our roe regulations. They also checked to be sure our crew passed U.S. regulations of no more than 25% Norwegian crew aboard. It was a close call with the bottles, but we passed inspection.

Steaming onward toward Dutch Harbor, we pulled in 140 tons of pollock. Every bag we hauled back yielded over 100 tons of fish. That day, the Bering Sea was calm, its flat, shining surface smooth as silk. On such days, it was easy to forget how easily the seas could change quickly to fury. The respite was nearly always short-lived. In six more days, we'd be back to port and already the waves and wind were beginning to shift. The water was getting choppy. My mood was shifting too. I was feeling twinges of homesickness and missing the Tuesday morning breakfasts I had regularly with my dad. I had just phoned him to wish him a happy birthday. Back then I also smoked and was running low on cigarettes. I was down to 2 ½ packs of cigarettes to last me six days, with no way to replenish them. The boat store was sold out. Also, I wasn't the only one aboard feeling edgy and unsettled. A gloom hovered around other crew because they felt there were too many techs on board, and they'd be making less money. You could feel the tension, it was so thick. But as we passed by a snow-covered volcanic island, its resplendent glacial beauty rising from the water, my breath stopped. The stunning natural beauty of the surrounding landscape instantly lightened my mood, as it always did. To ease my nerves, I decided, once-and-for-all, to go down to the factory and learn about roe processing.

Once down below, I learned our roe yield was much larger than our sister ships, the *Heather Sea* and *Claymore Sea*, and we were pushing hard to get it processed. The value of our share would earn me $8,000 in a mere three weeks of work, which was as much money as I'd been making at home in a year. The price of roe was very elevated, and I was elated! As it turned out, though, our yield of 100 tons of fish every two hours, when a normal rate was 80 tons per five or six hours, proved to be too much for the factory. Some of the fish turned bad. We suffered a lot of waste.

Chuck had been moved to a job on the surimi line, "driving," or putting the fish in a BAADER machine to remove their heads and gut them. The faster he processed the fish, the more money he would make. The seas were getting rougher, with 60-70 knot gale winds, so his job became very challenging. But, despite the pitching, as the enormous waves wrapped us and seemed to swallow up the boat, we were catching so much fish that the roe was turning green from the fish's bladder. We couldn't process it fast enough.

Our BAADER, or fish processing line and facility, was run by a Norwegian BAADER tech, Borger, who had started his fishing career when he was fourteen years old. I called him "Borger, the Seagull Herder" because when seagulls would get into the boat, he'd herd them down the passageways. He often told me stories about Norway and its culture, which helped to fill those endless hours of waiting to get to port. That said, we were all exhausted. Alongside exhaustion, egos also often ran high. Bobbi, our new First Cook, continued to condescend to me in her tone and manner. I found myself counting down the days until we reached port. Meanwhile, talk of maybe fishing on the Oregon coast or going to Russia began to circulate throughout boat.

With only three more days left until port, it began to snow, making the deck very slippery. I went up on the Bridge, the command area of the boat, to watch a haul back. Fishing was slow because we were surrounded by a lot of boats. While there, I reflected on what John, the 1st cook, had asked me, "Did I have interest in being promoted to 2nd Cook?" There would be more work and heavier responsibility, but Lee Magee, the current 2nd Cook, was leaving after our next trip. This meant I could test being a 2nd cook for one trip to see if I liked it. I'd get 2 ½ shares, which meant I'd be guaranteed $7,500. Additionally, I'd be given a break guarantee, based on trip yield, which was always more during roe season. I told John I wanted to give it a try. Pending office approval, I would be promoted. This was the beginning of my rapid climb up the corporate ladder and drove me to work that much harder.

Living through frigid winters [caption: With my daughter, Shana, and Jamie, the cook. The snow was blowing sideways in Dutch Harbor.

View from my porthole at Captain's Bay, Alaska.

With John Bloomfield, Chief Steward; Ariid Vatso, Fishmaster; and Adres,
Factory Manager at the Dutch Harbor airport heading home.

Dutch Harbor in winter.

Ice flows slow the *Saga Sea*.

The winters were bitter cold at Captain's Bay, Unalaska.

Nap time on the deck.

Ice flows hold the ocean down in the Bering Sea even when fierce winds blow.

Nautical Blackouts and
Other Disturbances

At 4:00 A.M. on January 13, 1991, I experienced an alarming moment, which I would later learn was commonplace. However, that night was my first fright, and very spooky and scary. I woke out of a deep sleep to hear someone yelling through the public address (PA) system, "Captain Kurt, can you hear me," followed by, "Everyone stay where you are!" I jumped out of bed to complete darkness. All the lights were out, and engine was dead. I had no idea what was happening. Chuck was sleeping on my couch, so I felt my way through the darkness and woke him. Feeling my way to our clothes, we both got dressed and were ready to run. For half an hour, the boat was dead in the water in complete darkness. The stark quiet was deafening, and then the lights went back on. But, by morning they were off again, and the boat was again dead in the water. On closer inspection, we discovered a wire on one of the nets had broken loose, rendering the boat stuck in the water. Since the boat hadn't been moving at all the sea strainers that cool the main engine had clogged up with fish guts and scales from the factory. Normally, seawater is sucked up through the engine to cool it. We weren't moving, so the waste from the factory had clogged the engine cooling system. This would not be my last blackout on a factory fishing boat, but it was certainly the most memorable because it had been the first.

That night, a Polish crew mate slipped in the factory and broke his shoulder, wrist, and arm. He suffered a bad concussion and we had to medivac him off the boat. Watching him lifted on a stretcher off our bow to a hovering helicopter and seeing the same doctor come aboard that had attended John gave me a chill. It was reminiscent of that fateful day John had died, as well as a poignant reminder of how dangerous the work we were doing was for all of us. Thankfully, however, we would learn later that the Polish guy lived to tell the tale.

Later that evening looking down from the wheelhouse, I watched deck hands hauling in fish through a raging storm. Violent waves reared over the back of the ramp, covering them with torrents of icy seawater as the boat leaped and pitched around them. One false step on the wet deck could have sent any one of them sliding dangerously across it. As I watched those deck hands haul that fish in under those fiercely treacherous conditions, I thought of how challenging it had been for me to just learn how to filet a fish. Despite not liking to eat it myself, I learned that if I was to ever advance my job to 2nd Cook, I'd have to learn to filet fish. So, even though their bulbous eyes made me squeamish, by the end of my first season fishing, I'd learned to filet a relatively small Ocean Pacific Perch. My next step would be to tackle a 30-pound cod, cutting it down its ribcage, chopping off its head, and avoiding its stinky, nasty stomach. Cod, being a bottom-feeder, always had a muck of food, cans, and other unmentionables in their stomachs.

When we finally reached Dutch Harbor, the weather outside was inhospitable, snowing, and freezing cold. Chuck was seasick again, so he was assigned to work indoors in the galley. Meanwhile, I was off-loading boxes of fish into "trampers," or delivery trucks used in long distance deliveries, in a freezing snowstorm. The wind chill factor made the temperature about five degrees. I couldn't see through the snow, but it was so cold, it hurt to open my eyes anyway.

In the middle of feeling somewhat miserable, I learned that Chuck and I, and the rest of our crew, were going to be featured in a *National Geographic* Magazine article about the Northwest fishing industry. We were both feeling sick and very tired, and though the prospect was exciting, we hardly felt camera-ready. Off-loading had also left a mess in the galley. The weather was also so nasty, all port operations shut down.

The next morning, January 18, 1991 was an astonishing day. As I've mentioned, Norwegians are highly superstitious about leaving port on a Friday, and to my amazement, we left port on a Friday. It was extremely rough on the water that day, and we were headed into an even worse storm. The sea that night was the worst I'd experience yet. I spent the entire night worrying about whether I'd be thrown from my top bunk. The next morning during a haul back of 150 tons of fish, a strap broke loose just as a bag loaded heavy with fish was being pulled up the stern ramp. It came crashing down on the deck. Luckily, no one was hurt, but the noise was deafening and scared me to death. A safety meeting and discussion about the importance of production followed. We were already ¾ full, so the captain said if we sped up production, we'd make significantly more money than he'd originally projected. He stressed the importance of working efficiently, fast, but safely.

The following day, the weather shifted and cooperated. Our fishing was good, and the sun came out. With luck, we'd be done by early February.

When you're out at sea, often the simplest things you take for granted at home become a luxury. I was looking forward to showering off the boat. Chlorine in the water was so strong it stung my eyes as I bathed. Though our engineers worked hard to understand why the chlorine was so powerful, it kept getting stronger. We also often ran out of toilet paper aboard. One time, Arild, our Fish Master, had to radio a sister ship, *Claymore Sea*, with an "S.O.S. toilet paper emergency." The *Claymore Sea* responded by dropping two garbage bags full of toilet paper into the ocean, attaching them to a buoy. We had to use a gaffing hook to retrieve our toilet paper from the water.

Something that might be a minor distraction on land can also prove to be very dangerous at sea. One day, Arild was so busy hauling in a huge bag of fish that he forgot to check his radar. We nearly hit another boat, which steamed past us, 100 yards off our starboard side. A "fender-bender" on land is regrettable, but likely not fatal. But between boats on the Bering Sea, a collision would have been monumental. I was grateful we didn't hit the other boat.

The sea was so turbulent the next day that I lost all the juice out of my machines. Food flew around the galley. After a long day of battling to stay upright, I went to John's cabin and partied with him and Bob, our First Mate, and Natalie, the *National Geographic* photographer, who had by that time come aboard to write her feature story about us. Natalie and Bob drank beer, while I drank tea. This brief respite was timely because the next day we entered even rougher seas with gale storm winds of 90-miles-an-hour. I slid all over the galley getting dinner out. As I sat to have a cup of tea, my chair catapulted across the galley and I slammed hard against the wall. Salad dressing sailed through the air and salad covered the floor. I slipped and slid very fast into the corner of the bulkhead, splitting my shin and wrenching my neck. I hit the floor so hard that I was in shock. The following day, the waves and wind had calmed down a little, but I felt as though I'd been hit by a truck. I hobbled around wounded for the rest of the day. With five more days until port, the rough weather was not behind us, and we were heeled over on a starboard list, which always made my job harder. That day, the hours crept by.

National Geographic photographer Natalie Forbes came aboard the *Saga Sea* to take photos of crew for a story.

Deckhand chipping ice off the deck of the *Claymore Sea*. The arm of the crane is above them covered in ice.

Housekeeper Kristin and Galley Assistant Judy Haglund on the bow of the *Claymore Sea*. Too much ice will sink the boat.

/ This is how we released tension on the *Saga Sea*! /

Promotion to Second Cook

Captain Kurt and I were becoming good friends. I'd periodically go up to talk with him in the wheelhouse. His boating experience intrigued me. His family had always had boats, he'd attended a Marine Academy for high school, and he'd crewed on the first trawler to fish for pollock in 1986. He told me *Saga Sea* was one of only a few boats that would be allowed to fish in Russia the following season. The fishing, he said, was going to be great there because the Russian trawlers stopped fishing at 8:00 p.m. In my next fishing contract, I'd be flying to Russia.

On a cold, snowy day as we pulled into port in Dutch Harbor, I started work as the 2nd Cook. It was such a relief to not have to be in the mess hall anymore. To celebrate, that night I caught a ride to the UniSea Bar, where again, I was the only person not drinking. Half of our crew was there getting drunk, including those who were scheduled to start work at 2:00 A.M. Some were too drunk later to work, while others slept through their shift. Ten people were fired that night. The next day, I had to manage the galley alone.

In the days that followed, the fishing was exceptionally good, but the weather was unpredictable. One day, while I was sitting in a lawn chair on the veranda soaking up sun during a break, within 20 minutes the sky darkened, and it began to snow. Then, the following day, we were out again on the deck basking in the sunshine. Looking out my porthole that night, the blackened sea was bathed in blinking lights from numerous other fishing vessels. In that dark span over the water, the lights looked like a bustling city filled with nightlife.

Steaming into the Pribilof Island area off the mainland of Alaska in the Bering Sea, I was hoping the crew would have some time off. Averaging four to five hours of sleep in 24-hours, they were so tired. I was bushed too, but still found energy to organize the storage area, which had been a mess. Then I headed up to the bow deck where John was waiting for me with a refreshing cocktail and the sun was shining. Relaxing in our lawn chairs, we could see volcanoes to the south.

The next day, after steaming all day to the north, the weather turned suddenly very cold. Gazing out my porthole, I shivered. Ice had gathered on the inside of it and we were steaming through drifts of solid ice fields. Since fishing trawlers aren't designed to cut through ice, moving through the ice fields was painfully slow. The water is dead calm. Usually I liked the fields, other than the relentless, grating sound of ice crunching against the ship's hull as it thrust ahead. The pace was so sluggish, we could easily step off the boat on to the surrounding frozen landscape, take photos, and then climb back aboard. But today, I had no interest in going out on to the ice. Relishing a few last minutes in bed, I felt a pang of loneliness and alienation. Though people came to the *Saga Sea* from all walks of life, one of the commonalities among both men and women aboard was a fondness for drinking to excess. Drinking was a big part of being socially accepted on board. A core group of women who were as rough-and-tumble as the men in their off-color jokes, brazen language, bantering, and heavy partying drove this behavior. Roger had once called the women of this core group "Alpha women." If these women decided to alienate someone from the core group for any reason, you would never be included in the inner circle. By some grace, I was considered a member of this inside group. But it was still a very tough place to stay sober. I had, but some of the people I'd met on land in Alcoholic Anonymous meetings lost their resolve when fishing. I was determined to stay the course, but sometimes it was hard.

As Second Cook, I had to learn to filet cod. John taught me how. They were huge at 40-pounds, with gelatinous bellies, and often still wiggling when I stuck the knife in them. I did not enjoy fileting them. Mutilating the fish and cutting up its face was disgusting to me, but it was part of my job. Crispy, deep-friend cod tongue and cheeks were a delicacy, and cooked Norwegian-style, a favorite meal among crew. They loved it.

On April 26, 1991, after two wonderful months at home in Seattle, I returned to Dutch Harbor. We sailed 30 minutes later. This time, Bobbi and I were training all the new galley people, including a few that didn't speak English. Trying to accomplish all my work as well as train the others, particularly with the language barrier, was a huge burden. Fishing was also slow. The sun wasn't setting until well past midnight, making sleeping at night difficult. I was restless. Something was amiss on board, too. Rumor had it that we had been fishing in a restricted area and entered an off-limits zone near Round Island in Bristol Bay.

About 20 miles outside Dutch Harbor, the National Marine Fishing Service (NMFS) called us back. *Saga Sea* was investigated, and the rumor proved to be true. The NMFS did not take kindly to our infraction. The Alaska Department of Fish and Game rigorously protected Round Island habitat and prohibited fishing anywhere near the protected area. Up to 14,000 male walruses had been known to congregate at Round Island for several days to feed. Seabirds, sea lions, and other marine birds and mammals also frequented its jagged, rocky, environmentally protected terrain. The area was a sanctuary and *Saga Sea* had violated its fishing regulations.

Emerald Resource Management, Inc. was fined $35,000 for altering the ship's log and lost a lot of money due to wasted time. We had to plead guilty to a felony account and a few people even went to jail. Later, the *Saga Sea* would have to pay the Russian government 15% of our gross product rather than money, equaling $600,000 worth of food. But, by May 5th, we were headed back to the new fishing grounds. That day, I cleaned my porthole, opened it, and leaned out into the crisp air. My room was on the port side, so the sun shone against my face. Listening to the waves splash against the boat was deeply peaceful. With no sight of land or other boats anywhere, the horizon stretched out, pristine and uncluttered, as far as I could see in all directions.

Bunking down that night, I slept so soundly, I overslept. The next morning, I had to prepare breakfast for crew in 15-minutes. Mike, our First Cook, and my roommate, had leg cramps and high blood pressure, so a medical professional radioed that he needed to take 36-hours of time off. This left me short-handed in the galley. If his health didn't improve, it was likely I'd be moved up to First Cook. Then we received news that Bobbi's mother had suffered a heart attack, so Bobbi chartered a float plane to Kodiak. The company then flew her from Kodiak back to Seattle. Though I felt bad for her personally, she'd been difficult as a boss. It was a happy day when Bobbi left the boat. Numerous people breathed a sigh of relief when she left, including me. Mike took over as acting Chief Steward. I really liked working with him. And, I never saw Bobbi again.

In 1991, I received a perfect score on my employee evaluation from *Saga Sea's* Chief Steward, Mike Hill. Since my supervisor, Bobbi, had left the company two weeks prior, I'd had to take over her responsibilities. Mike wrote, "My job would have been more difficult without Sindi assisting me. She is a great asset to this company." Alongside this evaluation, was a recommendation for an employee status change. Citing my skills in organization and training staff, I was to be promoted to 2nd Cook, despite one comment from one of my other supervisors about how I should utilize my spare time cooking or planning meals rather than socializing with crew. Occasionally socializing with crew is what kept me sane during those long, grueling work shifts. This was not a habit I planned to break. I needed social down time.

Steaming toward Bristol Bay on the eastern side of the Bering Sea in Southwest Alaska, barren mountains jutted out of the water around us. Reaching the harbor, we hooked up to a Japanese tramper. Val of Quality Control and I decided we wanted to tour a sea processing boat that was docked next to it. To get there, we had to crawl across a flexible hanging ladder connecting us to the Japanese trawler, which was made of vertical ropes and round, wooden rungs. Hanging on as this as this "Jacob's Ladder" as it swayed and wobbled beneath me, I very carefully edged myself across the spans. Once aboard the tramper, the Japanese crew was very hospitable. They gave us orange juice and boxes of fresh fruit. Then next to the trawler, tied to the port side of the tramper, was the *Royal Sea* processing boat we wanted to see. To get there, we had to crawl into a crane man basket that was surrounded by a cargo net. Arching high into the air, the crane lifted us over to the *Royal Sea*.

After a brief break from fishing and a quick visit to Seattle, John, Shana (my daughter), and I were headed back to Anchorage. Due to our plane's mechanical failure, and since the boat wouldn't be in Dutch Harbor for a few days, we decided to stay overnight in Anchorage. Our bags went on to Dutch Harbor without us. That night we went to Anchorage's iconic bar, Chilkoot Charlie's. With six separate bars boasting nearly 1,000 seats and sawdust on the floor of every one of them, it looked like a giant log cabin. A rustic place with cheap beer pitchers, it was a popular stopover for seafarers. Some of the seats were even converted tree stumps. In January 1970, when the establishment opened, it quickly became known for its easy vibe and raucous fun. The place drew national attention and attracted big acts like Lynard Skynard and Crosby, Stills, Nash and Young.

After a long night of fun there, the next morning, we rolled out of our beds and boarded a plane for Dutch Harbor. However, 2 ½ hours later when the plane couldn't land, we were routed back to Anchorage. By the time we finally got to Dutch Harbor, we were wearing the same clothes we'd had on for three days.

Our first day out, the waves were wild. I'd heard that the seas of Russia are among the roughest in the world, and that day I believed it. For four days, we were tossed around ferociously in stormy, high seas. The weather was also frigid. We worked very hard, 12-13 hours a day. In the middle of this tempest, our sister boat, the *Heather Sea*, tried to tie up to us. With a heavy clank, she boomed against the *Saga Sea*, nearly ripping a hole in our port side. Amid the flurry aboard, our first mate raced through the third deck, checking for damage to our rooms. Finding none, we systematically returned to our workstations. Alongside this excitement, Shana was seasick, sore, not up to speed yet, and starting to get snippy with me. I don't think she believed me when I warned her about how intense the work would be on the *Saga Sea*. John was also becoming frustrated with her lackadaisical attitude about work. Roger had said to me once that when you board a fishing trawler to work, all interpersonal relationships are secondary to being crew. This was even true of me as a mother with my daughter aboard. I told John to go ahead and rachet her attitude down a few notches if he needed to and give her a reality check. This was the "real world" and I was a proponent of tough love aboard. I assured him that it would not affect our friendship if he disciplined her. In fact, I said it might even help her understand that I was her boss, not her mom, in that environment. John held his patience for a while but after Shana disappeared from the galley twice and she kept arguing with him, he finally had words with her. Tears followed, but after that, her attitude and work improved immeasurably. It was smooth sailing from then on. However, we had both learned something vital from that fractious moment about work aboard a commercial fishing vessel. Every person aboard is an important part of the whole and needs to give 100 percent. Giving less than that hurts everyone.

That night, the mood between us had lightened. John, Shana, and I teased each other in the galley. I laughed so hard my sides ached. With Shana's help, I made Chinese food. Also, one of the deck hands brought us a King Crab to steam up. Dinner was delicious. The next day, Wednesday, November 20, 1991 marked my three-year anniversary of being sober. It felt good to be alive.

Alongside the fun, fishing was very bad, which meant it was likely we'd be out for an exceedingly long trip. We'd paid the Russian fisheries a lot of money for permission to fish in their waters and now we had no fish. It was very discouraging. Turbulent waves and foul winds were tossing the boat around, slamming us all over the galley. Shana took her first tumble, crashing to the floor with her salad, sliding across the galley. It scared her to tears, but John and I guffawed a little because Shana, covered in soggy lettuce and smashed tomatoes, was now officially "inducted" as a galley assistant.

By late November, the fishing improved. Since out of a fleet of 72 boats, we were among only five boats fishing at the time, due to the lack of fish, land canneries and fish processing plants had shut down. This made the fish we were catching a lucrative commodity. However, in December, we would catch two sea lions in our nets. The Russian fisheries didn't seem to care, but the emotional price we sometimes paid to catch the fish broke my heart.

That night at dinner, a crew member whose room was under the bow on our port side said saltwater was leaking into his room and the chain locker at the bottom of the boat was filled with water. Engineers and deck hands were speeding around trying to find the leak, to no avail. I was scared to death. Shana stayed in my room that night. We were listing badly to the port side and the seas were rough. I thought we were going to sink, so I packed my money and passport in my pockets, took down the photo of my dog, Sophie, from the wall, held on to it, and slept in my clothes. We were continuing to take on water, and a cracked hull was a possibility. About 3:00 A.M. that night, they located the problem. One of the ballast tanks in the bow filled with water because the pump hadn't been working. We all breathed a sigh of relief. At times like this, such as deaths at sea, crew had learned to just move on after an emergency and go back to work. But John was cranky and unreasonable the next day. To complain about his behavior today, I would have had to file a grievance, send an electronic grievance over a computer to the on-land central office in Seattle, wait for a response, work through a Human Resources negotiator, and then wait again for the resolution. The process would have taken days. But back then, we addressed tensions head-on, face-to-face. I had a talk with John and told him I felt he was being irritating, moody, unreasonable, and how I believed everything had to be his way or no way at all. We resolved my concerns long before they had any chance to become a real issue. That straight-on way of handing disputes and disagreements immediately saved a lot of time and hard feelings. Going forward, when I was having a moody day, I'd hang a sign on my cabin door. It read, "Gone fishing."

One of the underlying principles aboard commercial fishing vessels was about who you knew, not what you knew. Though this was also true of business and industry on land, out to sea it was pronounced. One first mate's girlfriend came aboard and during her first and only fishing trip, was trained to be a surimi quality control manager, bumping a few other experienced people from the opportunity. It wasn't fair, but it was how the politics worked. Another given was that sleeping arrangements were fluid. One amply sized married couple I knew cuddled together tightly in a very narrow single berth, and my roommate was sleeping with Borgeir, the BAADER Chief. Everyone was assigned to a bunk, but that didn't necessarily mean that was where they slept.

Straddling my fishing life with my home life always proved challenging. That December, a tree fell on my house. There was nothing I could do about it from sea. That same year on Friday, December 13th, we suffered the worst storm I'd experienced yet. We were slammed around the galley all day long. Food, pots, pans, dishes, and more were flying off the shelves in all directions, creating a colossal mess. At one point, John slid across the galley full speed and hit the cabinet so hard, he put a dent in it. The force brought tears to his eyes. I had never seen such stormy conditions. The Russian fleet had pulled all their boats in, the weather was so bad. The storm created such confusion, John thought he'd lost the potatoes he'd planned to cook for dinner. Turns out, he'd already put them in a frying pan. The next day, he received the sobering news he was going home, ostensibly because there had been food complaints and he'd lost his temper when someone stole his television. That had been what the First Mate and Captain told us. John's room had been our nightly stop for television, so the TV was a social center for many of us. It made sense that he would have been upset by its theft. But when we found a microtape recorder with a conversation between the First Mate, Captain, and John recorded on it and it was revealed that both the Captain and First Mate had denied having any complaints about John, we realized they had both lied to us about why John was leaving. None of us ever learned why. Our First Cook, Jayme, who knew little about John's job, would be taking his place as Chief Steward, working 24-hour shifts until a First Cook could be hired and brought aboard. She had her work cut out for her.

That same day, a bearing failed in one of *Saga Sea's* engines, so we had to drift until something could be done about it. Our engineers managed to jury-rig a bearing, so we could hobble our way back to port, stopping first to share fuel with our sister fishing trawlers, *Heather Sea* and *Claymore Sea*. As *Heather Sea* began to pull away, Tony, John, Jayme, and I watched, horrified, as she started banging our boat, her bow nearly piercing my cabin window. Running out of the room, I heard a powerful crunch of metal as *Heather Sea* swiped the port side of our boat, knocked our crane off, cracking a forward window, and pushing in our hull. I was terrified.

As much as senior crew would have liked to imagine sexism was not at play on board, it simply was a problem. In late December 1991, Shana was in a boy's room when an assistant foreman thought it would be funny to take the master keys from the Captain, open the door and snap a photo of them. I was incensed! It was such an invasion of privacy to know anyone could get master keys at any time and burst into a room like that. Frank assured me he'd get the film and return it to me, as well as write up the assistant foreman for his inappropriate behavior. But for as stressful as that situation was, that night John, Lorena, and Shana had a food fight in the galley. As it always did, the food fight worked off some of that angry steam. I filmed the entire bit of fun. Later that evening when all the crew was there, John dumped an entire bowl of chocolate pudding on my head. Everyone had a hearty laugh, and Shana caught it on film. I was going to miss John a lot. Somehow, I couldn't imagine food fights in Jayme's galley. The next day when we got into port, I took John to the airport. We hugged each other thoroughly, crying on each other's shoulders. He got such a raw deal. The *Saga Sea* galley wasn't going to be the same without John.

Christmas Eve, 1991, we had a busy day in the galley making Christmas cookies, fudge and hors d'oeuvres. Since Norwegians celebrate Christmas on Christmas Eve, we had a gift exchange. The BAADER Chief gave me a Norwegian troll doll from Norway. Tony gave me a copy of a song he'd written on his last trip. We opted to serve brunch instead of breakfast the next morning. I was so exhausted.

The next morning, about 20 of us, including Norwegian officers, climbed off the boat to go sledding, trudging up a mountain through snow up to our knees. We took fish meal bags and cargo nets with us. The hill we climbed had a vertical drop, so our sledding was both scary and fun. Everyone but me was also drunk, so it was rowdy and rambunctious, too. As we plunged down the steep incline, high winds whipping around us, snow flurries nipping across our faces, it was an unbelievable blast!

Back aboard, as we started steaming out of port, we hit a raging storm with 80 mile-an-hour winds so forceful they blew out a window on the Bridge and the bow filled with water. All I heard that night was SLAM! BANG! CRASH! BOOM! Our radar system failed. Finally, conditions were so bad that we had to turn away from the storm. In a brief, calm moment the next day, I had just enough time to organize our storage. Chief Steward Jayme was trying to get me a raise or promote me to First Cook. We'd been out for four days and only caught 70 tons, so I was welcoming the notion of a raise/promotion. Shana was acting up again and we were barely speaking. I was concerned her behavior was going to also reflect badly on me and get me into trouble. She tended to leave salad contents in the sink drains, and after reminding her of it for the umpteenth time, I finally threw an errant radish at her. This began a radish game between us. She put the radish in my laundry bag. I stealthily went into the galley and plopped it into her sink of dishes. When I went back to my cabin that night and was washing my face, that same radish came rolling toward me. For four hours, we passed the radish back and forth until finally we had a good laugh about it. Yes, there was no question she had my DNA. I was glad for that fun moment, albeit born of frustration, because the next day we learned Shana was being sent home because the fish master's girlfriend was coming up to work in the galley as an assistant. Nepotism always ruled aboard the boat, but in truth, I think Shana was feeling ready to go home.

Jayme, the First Cook who had temporarily replaced John as Chief Steward, was loading me up with most of her work, which was weighing heavily on me. It was also bitterly cold outside, and the boat was bone-chillingly cold. It was New Year's Eve and the galley had lost its charm without John. This would be the 2nd time I'd greet the new year aboard *Saga Sea*.

That morning, Roger, our Head Engineer, came into my room. A swarthy, handsome Norwegian with crystal blue eyes, he had a slight reputation as a lady's man. But he was also very smart, kind-hearted, and the brains of the boat that kept us afloat. At first, I woke with alarm because he was dressed in a freezer suit, which was a bulky, insulated garment designed for extremely cold conditions. I thought something was terribly wrong and that I would be soon leaping into foul weather gear myself. As it turned out, he just wanted to let me know he hadn't been asleep yet because he'd been fixing frozen winches on the boat. Grinning, I told him that the least he could do for startling me was to bring me a cup of coffee. When he brought the cup of coffee back to me and I looked over the rim of the mug at him, I thought to myself, "Now, there's a very good Norwegian. Happy New Year!" We had a lot of fun fueling a rumor that Kevin, our Assistant Engineer, started about us for fun. After delivering fresh-baked cookies to the engine room and control room, I took coffee to Roger every morning. One morning prior to Shana leaving Saga Sea, Roger accidentally poured acid on his hand. He asked Shana to get me, so loud as day over the loudspeaker during mealtime, she announced, "Mom, Roger wants you!" I could hear a titter spread through the mess hall. I could have died! So, I went to his room to help him clean up. That stuff can easily burn your skin off. While Roger was in the shower, Fish master Arne knocked on the door, and when I opened it, there in plain sight was Roger showering in my room. Rumors flew rampant the next day! By late January 1992, we'd become close friends.

One night I came back to my cabin after a long day's work. I locked my door, as I always did when I took a shower, and after showering, crawled into bed. Roger would check on me every night before retiring to his cabin. That night he knocked on my door and I didn't answer. When he discovered my door was locked and I wasn't answering, he was alarmed. He said he very nearly used a master key to come in and check to be sure I was okay. As I did every morning, I took him his daily cup of coffee to wake him up. He was so happy to see his "human alarm clock" was okay, he jumped up out of bed and gave me a huge hug.

Another night while we were in port, Roger invited me to dinner. When I accepted and asked where we were going, he told me he had some King Crab he planned to steam up. So, I took melted butter, a fresh lemon, a loaf of homemade bread, and orange juice to Roger's cabin. He arrived about ½ an hour later. We had a spectacular feast! The next morning, Roger brought me coffee and the bantering and genuine caring of each other that came later sealed a friendship that abides to this day.

I had another friend, Tony. We often watched television together. He was like a brother to me, and we both agreed neither one of us would leave before the other. Eventually, though, he missed his wife and kids too much and went home. I missed his company on board a lot.

We reached port the next day and I received the unsettling news that Charlie's brother, Willy, had suffered a stroke and was on life support. It was unimaginable to think of the world without Willy. He was such a great guy. On this occasion, and many more to follow, I would poignantly realize that I was missing big moments in the lives of people I loved; birthdays, marriages, babies being born, and deaths. Feeling isolated, numb, and helpless was one of the consequences I would frequently bear during my fishing career. I decided to fly home to Seattle to check on Willy. He was in a deep coma. I had breakfast with Dad, Helen, Charlie, and Bobby. It felt great to touch down with family. Later that month, Willy would pass away. I was glad I'd had the chance to say good-bye.

The Tundra Mountains in Dutch Harbor, Alaska.

Claymore Sea days, Dutch Harbor, Alaska.

Crab feast at the Grand Aleutian Hotel Restaurant with crew in Alaska.

Fishmaster Eric barbecuing on the beach at Pier One, West Seattle, Washington.

/ Me holding "Red Fish" or Pacific Ocean Perch (POP), Alaska. The bigger the fish, the older they are - I have seen them over 20 years old. /

/ Me taking a break on deck. /

Promotion to First Cook

A few days later, I reconnected with the *Saga Sea*. We had 140 people on board to feed! It was such a zoo. The night before we left port, Jayme was fired. No one knew why. Terri, a former First Cook, became Chief Steward. I was elevated to First Cook, which meant I was making $125 per day, which by today's standards was worth a guarantee of nearly $250 a day. I was still working lunch but also doing the meal planning for 140 people.

Captain Kurt, who was the captain of *Saga Sea* when I first started fishing, had been demoted to the *Heather Sea*. It was common knowledge to everyone but him that he was only aboard for his license and that the Norwegian Fishmaster would be overseeing the fishing. Just 24-hours before the *Heather Sea* started fishing for pollock roe in the Bering Sea, Captain Kurt realized he had no jurisdiction over his fishing trawler. Fed up with deferring to the Norwegian Fishmaster and with no interest in being told what to do with his boat, Captain Kurt turned *Heather Sea* around and headed back to Dutch Harbor, abandoning a lucrative catch. The Norwegian Fishmaster couldn't stop Captain Kurt because to do so would have meant he'd have had to admit he was commanding the ship, which was a violation of the U.S. law that required vessels fishing in U.S. waters to be skippered by a U.S. citizen. Some foreign-owned fishing companies ignored this law by hiring two sets of officers to command the wheelhouse and engine room aboard factory trawlers, with one set of officers doing the work and the others aboard for show only. The U.S. citizens had the titles and licenses to keep the law compliant, but little position once their vessels went to sea. Once back on shore, U.S.-born Captain Kurt told the Norwegian owner of the *Heather Sea* that he would not serve as a "paper captain." I was sad to hear this news. Captain Kurt had been a good friend to me, and it pained me to hear how he'd been treated. He'd deserved better.

As I neared the end of this fishing stint on the *Saga Sea*, the fish holding tanks began leaking into our fresh water, making cooking with fresh water impossible. Everything smelled like rotting fish. We had 25 pounds of fish stuck in one of our tanks that wouldn't pump out which was a serious problem. Roger had to crawl up into Tank 4 and cut a hole between Tank 3 and 4. The only way out was through a hatch. Memories of another hatch and the death aboard haunted me. I breathed a sigh of relief when I learned Roger was okay and that his savvy engineering had cleared the tank. With smooth sailing of 50 mile-an-hour winds and relatively calm, high seas, we steamed our way back to Dutch Harbor. In a very short while, I'd be headed home to Seattle. But it would not be before I made a crucial decision about what was to come next.

The Chief Steward of another trawler, the *Claymore Sea*, was leaving her job as Chief Steward. Captain Mark Sablick of the *Claymore Sea* had offered me the job. His First Cook had refused it which should have been a clue about whether I should accept it. But when I hesitated at his offer, Captain Mark had said, "I have no respect for anyone offered such a job who doesn't take it." Against my better instincts, I allowed him to convince me I would be making a big mistake to turn down his offer. But, as I would later find out, underlying that comment of "no respect" was a lurking a "no respect for women and specifically a confident woman." In retrospect, had Captain Mark been half the boss that he was salesman for that position, I'd have had a much better experience aboard The *Claymore Sea*. However, all I would learn from my time aboard the vessel would be how to stay one step ahead of a narcissist, keep my composure and forge ahead with stalwart resolve.

Fish holding tank on the *Claymore Sea*.

Captain Mark Sablick, *Claymore Sea*, playing Xbox during down time.

SECTION TWO:
ABOARD
THE *CLAYMORE SEA*

EMERALD RESOURCE, INC.

CHIEF STEWARD

SEPTEMBER 28, 1992 – NOVEMBER 8, 1996

Discrimination at Sea

Within minutes of stepping about the Claymore Sea, I was filled with apprehension and the sinking sense that I'd made a glaring mistake. Working aboard the vessel was a miserable experience. In truth, I really hadn't wanted the job anyway, but I'd let Captain Mark shame me into taking it. He'd insinuated I'd be less of a person if I turned it down despite what my gut was telling me. My willingness to let him shame me was my downfall. But it had been an opportunity to become a Chief Steward which was one I ultimately did want. So, despite my apprehension, I'd taken it. The money was good – and it was what kept me there, but the experience was rugged.

For one, the galley was not the pristine, shining example of culinary efficiency I'd enjoyed while working aboard the *Saga Sea*. Instead, the cooking space was so small, it was hard to imagine how more than one person could fit into it and cook for more than two people, much less an entire crew. It was tiny and cluttered with long, metallic shelving stretched on either side. An oven hung at the high end of it, encased in the wall. How was I going to feed dozens of hungry men from this "closest" of a galley? I had no idea. Going from the galley on the *Saga Sea* to the galley on the *Claymore Sea* was like going from the Hilton to a homeless camp, that's how markedly different the two ships were.

Plus, if the cramped quarters weren't enough to make the galley working conditions challenging, the vessel was also cockroach infested and the pests preferred the kitchen over other parts of the boat. Nothing was done to eliminate them. On several occasions, I had to physically kills roaches with my own hands in the laundry room and dry stores. To put it mildly, smashing them gave me the creeps and they did not die easily. There's a reason the myth developed that cockroaches will be the only living creature left on earth in the event of a nuclear apocalypse. Though this claim to fame isn't true, their crusty little bodies are nearly impossible to kill, and they scurry faster than any insect I've ever tried to catch. They come by this reputation of indestructibility honestly.

I remember taking a galley assistant over to the *Claymore Sea* while I was still working on the *Saga Sea*. She was shocked at the age and condition of the vessel, the oldest in our fleet. Going aboard the *Claymore Sea* was truly a harsh step back in time.

Additionally, my galley assistant was my ex-sister-in-law who was also a raging alcoholic. Captain Bob, the other captain and a friend of mine to this day, had confined her to the boat because she was never sober. However, despite her confinement, I could never figure out how she ended up drunk anyway. Come to find out, the Chief Advisor had a crush on her, so he was going into town and buying her alcohol. This was a very difficult boat.

Looking out my porthole that first night, I realized my former serenity of gazing out over pristine waterscapes was over too. Trawling through the Bering Sea aboard the *Claymore Sea* was a much rougher experience than it had been on the *Saga Sea*. Navigating rough waves and weather that first night, the *Claymore Sea* had started to roll to the left and then BOOM! I'd been thrown hard across my bunk as the ship's hull slammed flat against the water. Its aged structure had long since lost any ability to roll gently through the waves, if it had ever had that capability. Stabilizers flanking the vessel were meant to help keep it level during rough water but rather than rolling with the motion of the waves, the *Claymore Sea* continually slammed unmercifully against the water. BAM! BAM! BAM! This jarring movement not only sent people flying, it always caused havoc in the galley, with spinning food, pots, pans, flatware and dishes catapulting through the air. The galley was so small, though, it was possible to leap and catch the kitchen equipment as it flew by. During bad weather, the boat would rapidly roll, slam and shudder. This acrobatic feat of saving food and equipment became commonplace.

The most disturbing part of working on the *Claymore Sea*, however, was not the vessel. It was its captain. Shortly after I arrived, Captain Mark Sablick informed me that I would not be hired to work as the Chief Steward aboard the *Claymore Sea* after all. He'd learned that his friend, Howard, who was a Chief Steward from another trawler, was interested in the job. I was, therefore, expected to graciously step down from the offer. However, I'd already accepted the position, transitioned my life with that expectation, and been made a formal offer. I wasn't about to move over for his friend. This riled Captain Mark plenty. Years later, I would also learn that he also hated me because he'd been under the false impression that I felt entitled to be a "trouble-maker" because my cousin, Paul, was president of the company. Nothing could have been further from the truth.

From day one, however, Captain Mark would be at harsh odds with me. I would venture to say that 90% of my career harassment on the *Claymore Sea* was due to his deep resentment that I hadn't relinquished my position to his friend. Working for him in that caustic, hostile environment was horrendous. Beyond that, the men aboard the *Claymore Sea* were already a "testosterone-heavy boy's club." Navigating my way through that "club" with a measure of self-esteem was challenging. I had to constantly fight against a heavy weight of opposition regarding both my gender and my position.

Captain Mark was, to put it truthfully, a sexist jerk. He harassed me every chance he got. He also disliked the galley crew and made our life as tough as he possibly could. One time he blew pepper into a galley woman's face just to let her know who was boss. He was also noted for barging into female crewmates' cabins and blowing air horns into their faces to wake them up in the morning. Captain Mark was also best buddies with the Factory Manager, Joel Rae. When the crew size expanded from 102 to 126, I made a request for more help in the galley. The *Heather Sea* and *Saga Sea* both had an extra person, so it seemed like a reasonable request. Captain Mark's solution to my request was to hire Joel Rae's girlfriend, Michelle, who truly didn't even know how to tie her shoes, much less give me any substantive help. I was told that she was my "extra help" and was expected to accept that edict. I told Joel that she would be working for me, not him, and that she would not get any special privileges based simply on the fact that the two of them were sleeping together. Michelle was a problem employee from day one. She was late every day, it was difficult for her to follow instructions, and she had absolutely no respect for me. But, if I hadn't allowed this nepotism, however, both Captain Mark and Joel Ray would have made my life a living hell. Factory Managers had a lot of power on the trawlers. The only compliment I ever heard about my cooking from Joel was that "it was good but that must be because his girlfriend, Michelle, was helping me now in the galley." Michelle would later quit, stomping defiantly out of the galley because I spoke seriously to her about her incapacity to do her work. Joel Ray would inform me that since Michelle refused to work in the galley, I would have no help. In other words, unless his girlfriend was my assistant, no one would be. It was impossible to work with Michelle, however. I was not allowed to reprimand her, and she knew it. If I did try to discipline her, she ran to Joel, complaining that I was "picking on her." I finally decided Michelle was more trouble than she was worth and said, "fine." I would manage the galley on my own. Captain Mark, however, took objection with my decision. He suggested that I wasn't trying hard enough to resolve my problems with Michelle.

Sexual and emotional harassment also ran rampant. Female crew members complained about it, but in those days, these kinds of complaints were basically ignored. One of the foremen regularly took a female fish processor to a "secret place" to do what he wanted to do with her. No one said anything about it, including the abused woman. He had power. No one wanted to lose their jobs and he could fire them without just cause. Women certainly didn't have the legal protection in the workplace that they have now.

Dutch Harbor, located in the funky little port of Unalaska, was also always fun. Although I didn't drink, I often went ashore with those who did – and, when we did go, we always went to the now demised, once infamous Elbow Room. An icon of the town's fishing history, it was always packed with fisherman and crabbers releasing the stress of working under highly dangerous conditions day-after-day. From belly-sliding across its beer-covered floor to the flow of cocaine in the bathrooms and brawls that tumbled into the street, patrons of the Elbow Room made the place legendary. Fights, stabbings and shootings were regular occurrences there. But, often after tussling with each other outside, if they lived, they'd came back right inside to buy each other drinks. At one time the bar even had the reputation as being the most rough-and-tumble bar in the country. Before modern encroachment from paved roads and big box stores hit the area, the Elbow Room was an icon that represented Unalaska. It was casual, rough, and dank. A thirsty fisherman could feel comfortable trundling directly into the bar, smelly clothes and all. But despite its humble environment, those who frequented it had plenty of money to spend. During the crabbing boom of the 1980s, some boats were making a million dollars or more. With nowhere else to spend their money, deckhands often whirled in with rolls of $100 bills in their pockets ready to drink. At most bars in Alaska, "ringing the bell" meant that someone in the bar was buying the next round. But at the Elbow Room, people had so much money, they'd pay thousands of dollars to buy the bar for the entire night. On particularly busy nights, people chose to crawl on their hands and knees to get to the bar because it was faster than trying to weave their way through the throngs of people there. On one of those especially crowded nights, singer/songwriter Jimmy Buffet came into the bar. It was so crowded nobody saw him there until he got on stage.

By the time the Elbow Room closed in November 2007, it had been made famous by "Deadliest Catch" skippers who in season three of the show had placed a bet as to who could bring in the first 100,000 pounds of crab in the least number of pots. Some locals credit the demise of the Elbow Room with the fame it received from the show. One of our adventures in the bar involved a fishmate and fishmaster who got so drunk in its front room that I have no idea how we got them back onboard the *Claymore Sea* undetected. It was in the Elbow Room that I would again be recognized by someone from home who I'd once hung out with in Ballard, Rick Johnston. I'd known him since I was 17 or 18 years old. Back then, he'd come home from fishing with his pockets brimming with money.

Cooking crab aboard was a 'no-no' but we boiled them up anyway for special occasions like birthday parties. Joel Westgate (RIP), the "Silver-haired Fox" with crab.

Fish galore, *Claymore Sea*.

Judy, Kristin, and Gena making a birthday cake aboard the *Claymore Sea*.

Food prep in the galley of the *Claymore Sea*.

Aboard the
Claymore Sea.

Sitting by
the net reels.

Foreman Jeff,
down below in
the *Claymore Sea*
factory.

Me and Joel Westgate (RIP), the "Silver-haired Fox."

With Captain Bob of the *Claymore Sea*.

The freezer after a storm on the *Claymore Sea*.

Judy cleans the walk-in after a storm.

Food prep in the galley of the *Katie Ann*.

"I said, RISE!" Creating bread dough, *Katie Ann*.

The runway at Dutch Harbor, Alaska.

Looking out the porthole toward the trawl deck aboard the *Claymore Sea*.

Jeff Harmon, Foreman; Gena, Quality Control; and Judy (my ex-sister-in-law), Galley Assistant, on the *Claymore Sea*.

Captain Mark Sablick in the galley of the *Claymore Sea*.

Randal Lee crawling up the net to dump the bag of fish, *Claymore Sea*.

After the bag of fish have been released from the nets and down to the live tanks, *Claymore Sea*.

Kristin Kolgrov sorting fish during a kick shift in the *Claymore Sea* factory.

Processing roe during a kick shift on the *Claymore Sea* with my former sister-in-law, Judy.

Fun food fights aboard the *Claymore Sea* with Ove Kolqrov.

Ove holding a King Salmon, *Claymore Sea*.

Birthday feast on the *Claymore Sea* with me and Craig Anderson.

Slathered in a food fight on the *Claymore Sea*.

Pounding chicken in the galley with a BAADER tool on the *Claymore Sea*.

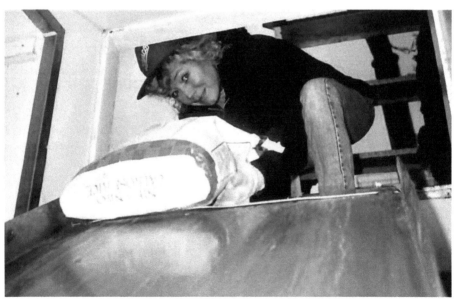

Backloading rice on the *Claymore Sea*.

Cooking on the *Claymore Sea.*

Many cakes were baked for birthdays and special occassions. Gena on her birthday.

/ Killer Whales join us along the voyage in the Bering Sea. /

Sometimes it was Just like Being in the Movies

As the *Claymore Sea* steamed into the Bering Sea, I remember one day that will never be forgotten by one of my fellow crewmates, Lau. He had no way of knowing that crisp day in November 1990 would be any different from the countless other days he'd been at sea. Normally, the swarthy Samoan had an even temperament that wasn't swayed by harsh winds and weather and took everything around him in stride. His wide smile and easy manner had made him a favorite among the *Claymore Sea* crew. But this day would test his mettle. It would be one that he would never forget.

As one of the ship's mechanics, Lau loved fixing equipment. Taking something broken and making it run again, particularly when the ship was far from land, gave him great satisfaction. He came by his fondness for it naturally. As a kid, he'd always loved tinkering with old radio parts and broken cars. His focused attention to making non-working parts function again hadn't altered with age, which is what made him so good at piecing together the live tanks that held fish after a catch been pulled off the ship's deck. That day, he'd been in the fish holding tank for a long time working on a series of broken bolts, but he wasn't concerned. He liked the slow pace of getting the job done right. His thick arms, tattooed with swords, fish, shells, and waterfalls in native Samoan fashion, rippled in the shadows. Humming a song from the old country to himself, Lau felt right at home hunkered down in that live tank, ratcheting its water flow pipe back into working order.

"There," he said with a deep breath triumphantly to himself, "it's done." Pulling himself from a crouched position, as he straightened his heavy bulk up to stand, to his horror, he heard the sudden crunch of a latch shutting as the lid above him closed tightly. He realized with a start that he was now locked in, held captive in the dark steel tank. Also, someone had not only thoughtlessly latched the tank, they had turned the water on, which burst in a sudden stream from the repaired pipe. If he couldn't get someone's attention, Lau knew that he was headed to a certain watery grave. Moreover, as water start to pour into the tank, and the tank filled around him, the walls also started to close in. This could only mean one thing. No one knew he was in the live tank. He knew the likelihood was that he'd either drown or be crushed by the closing walls – and it would happen very quickly.

Feeling as though he'd been dropped into the set of a horror film, a scene from the movie, "Indiana Jones and the Temple of Doom" in which Indiana Jones is in an ancient ruin that begins to close around him, flashed through Lau's mind. His normally bright, even smile turned into a tight grimace as he hollered out into the darkness, "HEY!! THERE'S SOMEONE IN HERE – OPEN THE LATCH NOW!!" But the silence was deafening as the water rose and the walls encroached closer. It was clear no one had heard him.

Frightened and alone in the dark, as the water reached his shoulders, Lau pondered why he had voluntarily put himself into a situation that could be so treacherous. But even in that terrifying moment he knew he was there because he loved fishing, the sea, and fixing things. When he'd first walked in the door of Emerald Resources, he had not been able to contain his enthusiasm for the job. They'd hired him on the spot. However now, with only seconds to go before he would be completely submerged by the flooding water shooting into the tank, Lau's life begun to flash through his mind. Had it been worth the risk? If so, how could this possibly be the end? He had only just turned thirty. By this time, Lau's usual even-keeled personality was rapidly escalating into one of sheer panic and desperation. The water was up to his chin. He started frantically yelling "help," and when that didn't work, screamed "fesoasoani" in the hopes that a fellow Samoan crew mate might hear him. For some inexplicable reason, hollering help in his native tongue seemed to comfort him in that dark, inhospitable chamber. He knew that unless someone heard him, he would either drown or be crushed by the closing tank walls – and, it was going to happen soon. The water had now reached his nose.

Suddenly he heard another crack and saw a thin shaft of light peeking into the darkness. To his relief, someone had heard him cry out. He was being lifted out of the tank from under his shoulders up onto the deck. The water had been turned off – and, none-too-soon. It could be said that this was just another day at sea. Accidents like this happened all the time. But for Lau, this day was one he would never forget. Lady Luck had smiled on him. Years later, the experience would still haunt his dreams.

But it would be another far less life-threatening but equally dramatic experience that would haunt my dreams for years to come, and it had to do with Captain Mark.

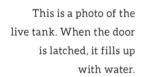
This is a photo of the live tank. When the door is latched, it fills up with water.

/ I would recount the
days in my personal journal /

The Journal Debacle

Hunkered down in my bunk, the *Claymore Sea* rocked heavy against high waves and weather. But I was sound asleep, dreaming of smooth seas and southern trade winds, my body long since adapted to the frequent pitching of the boat. Suddenly my reverie was blasted awake by the shrill shriek of a blow horn right next to my ear, sounding so suddenly that my heart raced uncontrollably. My eyes few open and there was the burly apparition of Captain Mark hovering over me. "Get up, Captain Sindi," he scoffed. He'd assigned this nickname to me because he knew I was not going to take any guff from him and that when pushed, I would stand up for myself. He enjoyed muscling his short, squat body and demeaning attitude over all the women aboard, especially me. Other mates had heard him more than once refer to me sarcastically as "Captain Sindi." It wasn't a compliment.

To say that Captain Mark sometimes harassed me and my staff, would be an understatement. We were constantly singled out and harassed. With a raucous, demeaning attitude toward women that would never pass in today's sexual harassment training workshops, he often told off-color jokes to the women on crew to see how they would respond. Thinking it funny to plague my galley crew, he would also wake them up from their bunks with a sudden, painful blast of blow horns in their ears. Other times he would require my staff to do kick-shifts (mandatory extra work hours) when no one was around and there wasn't any fish in the factory. He encouraged others to harass me, too and rallied his troops around him. Factory workers would always bring up food when I needed it. One time, a factory manager decided she needed the entire cargo space for the fish we'd been processing, so since she had Captain Mark's favor and I did not, she completely disrespected the fact I needed a portion of the cargo hold for my food. She had her processors unceremoniously dump my food in the middle of the galley. All of it. Not in the freezer hold, but right on the counter and the deck, blocking all access to the kitchen. Another time, Captain Mark had written up my galley staff and then decided better of what he'd said since much of it was fabricated and harassing. He ripped up the original documentation, deciding instead to change it before it went to the central office. On her own volition, my sweet Norwegian housekeeper took the scraps out of Captain Mark's trash and pieced it back together so I could see what he had initially written to the central office. It was complete fabrication.

Captain Mark's harassment was blatant, but unfortunately, that was the sign of the times. It's just how it was back then. Women were not respected – and it was horribly wrong, but it was allowed. Captain Mark's behavior was very passive aggressive but there was nothing I could do about it. After all, I was there for mealtime and I enjoyed the creative latitude my job gave me. Captain Mark knew his behavior was inappropriate, but he didn't care because he believed he could get away with it, protected by miles of open sea and those aboard who were afraid of his ill-temper. He openly despised me. One of the reasons he didn't like me was because I didn't drink. He often took crew to the beach to get all of them drunk. During those times, one bosun stayed onboard with me. Once onshore, Captain Mark's boozed blowouts would often break out into violent brawls, drunkenness, and the occasional stabbing. These were often followed by a surly, inebriated crew returning on board who would continue the fight on the ship. One such night, a particularly violent fight broke out that culminated in police swarming our boat. That night, Captain Mark took everyone but me and the deck boss, Joel, off the boat to get drunk. It was a recipe for disaster. Typically, Asian and Samoan crewmates did not get along – and, when ignited by alcohol, the tensions between them became even worse. So, a huge fight exploded aboard the boat. It was a horrible nightmare. My galley assistant, among many others who were injured, got stabbed. In seconds, everything was out of control. A swaggering Captain Mark and over a hundred staggering others were roaring drunk. Many of them were violently fighting.

"JOEL," I'd hollered as one of the drunk sailor's fists swiped past me barely missing my head, "What do we do now?" We were the only two sober people on the boat. It was so bad that our dock guy, the expeditor who stayed on the dock, wanted to cut our lines. So, in desperation, we called the harbor master, who upon realizing the situation had escalated beyond what he felt comfortable controlling, finally called the police.

No one was arrested that night, but the police did stay until everyone was settled down. It was a big deal. Lawyers were even involved – and Captain Mark was mightily steamed at me for making the ruckus public.

Eventually, the atmosphere at the *Claymore Sea* became so untenable that I decided to protect myself by journaling everything that was happening to me there. One day, Captain Mark found out that I was keeping a journal. I heard his voice call out over the ship's intercom, "Sindi Giancoli, to the wheelhouse now!" When I arrived, his arms were folded behind his back Napoléon-style and his chest jutted out authoritatively. He was pacing.

"Captain Sindi," he hollered, as his brow began to sweat and his eyebrows furrowed, "Give me that f-ing journal and you know which one I mean!" Afraid of what I might reveal in it which could potentially lose him his captain's license, Captain Mark knew he'd be in big trouble if the central office found out that he'd instigated drunken debacles, particularly ones that erupted in violence. He also rightfully suspected that I'd documented countless examples of his blatant harassment, also cause for his termination. I drew myself up and said emphatically, "Absolutely not! My journal is my personal property. Company policy forbids you from demanding I part with it simply because you want me to." I planted my feet firmly in front of him.

"That's an ORDER, Giancoli!! Did you hear me? That's an ORDER!" he furiously blurted out. We had a huge fight about it. Enraged, he stormed into my locker, attempting to steal it from me. But I'd already removed it, slipping it to my galley assistant, who'd hid it down her spandex and then given it to Joel, the bosun, for safekeeping. It was my personal property and I wasn't about to part with it, no matter how much Captain Mark screamed at me. He went on an arduous search for it for days but never found it. I am grateful he didn't find it because I've been referencing it to write this book. This action happened during the same time period that former Oregonian attorney and politician Bob Packwood argued that he should not have to turn over his personal diaries to an Ethics Committee because they were his private property. According to press reports at that time, Packwood had once pressured a lobbyist to give his ex-wife a job, ostensibly to reduce his pending alimony payments. It was believed this claim was mentioned by Packwood in his diaries. However, he was not on trial for that reason. He was being tried for sexual harassment. So, his argument was that he should not have to turn over his diaries to determine whether he had pressured the lobbyist because that was not why he was on trial. Since Packwood's trial was fresh in the news the time, I had his logic against turning over my personal diary to Captain Mark at the forefront of my mind. I used it to strengthen my case with a company lawyer and it was upheld, further infuriating Captain Mark. The matter was put to rest legally, but from that day on, every encounter with Captain Mark was highly unpleasant.

But even as wretched an environment as Captain Mark could make working on the *Claymore Sea*, and for as much harassment as I endured while I was there, it was not without some fun. One of the few joys I had while working on the *Claymore Sea* was that my "best-friend-forever" (BFF), Captain Bob, was aboard. We'd been friends from the *Saga Sea*. Due to our banter and true connection, buzz aboard was that Captain Bob and I were lovers. But that was never true. However, other crew members resented our friendship.

On the night of Captain Bob's birthday, he wasn't on watch, so we gave him a party and got him roaring drunk. At the same time in another part of the vessel, two female crew members had a complaint about harassment. Captain Rob Hempstead was looking for Captain Bob because claims of harassment required two captains for mitigation of the assertion. But Captain Rob couldn't find Bob. The reason was, of course, we'd boiled up king crab for Captain Bob's birthday party and were busy eating it and getting Captain Bob drunk. Serving crab was forbidden aboard trawlers - a big "no-no." But I must confess to having enjoyed it more than once. It always seemed like such a waste to toss dead crab back into the ocean when it could be steamed up for a party. I also remember baking a lot of wonderful birthday cakes that were themed with whatever the receiver's position was on the vessel. For staff who worked in the freezer hold, I decorated the cake with a rat dressed as a guy. Our nickname for people who worked in the freezer hold was "freezer rat." Or, if it was a bosun's birthday, I'd make a net across the cake.

One day, on my galley assistant's birthday, I was watching a catch being pulled in with the factory manager, Craig. Piled into the net was a heap of King Crab. I jokingly said to Craig, "I will put a pot of water on if you bring the crab." An hour later, there he was with a pile of King Crab! Though it was highly illegal to cook the crab and by law and we were supposed to just throw it back in the water, we hid it until we were able to secretly boil it. We then had a birthday party for my galley assistant, complete with cooked crab legs. Everyone but me got drunk. We all had a great time. Years later while looking through photos of that time, Captain Bob, who'd remained a good friend of mine, said, "I don't remember ever serving King Crab on the boat." He didn't authorize serving any. He could have lost his license as a captain if he had and it'd been discovered.

So, we did have some fun times to buffer the stressful ones. Today, I'm thrilled to write that after nearly fourteen years of fishing in the Bering Sea and North Pacific Ocean, though Captain Rob Hempstead never did find Captain Bob that night, he is now in charge of the Royal Caribbean International's newest and largest cruise ship, *Symphony of the Seas*. After years of braving those wild, death-defying conditions and rough weather fishing on factory trawlers, Captain Rob certainly earned this distinction fair and square. It could not have happened to a nicer guy.

Another happy memory I have of that time was my friendship with Joel Westgate, the "silver fox." We nearly became a couple but, at the time, he was married, and I was still dealing with a broken heart, which is another story for another time. But the "silver fox" and I remained very close friends until he passed away years later.

/ What awaits us ahead. /

Unjust Departure and
a Better Future

On the morning of January 11th, 1996, Eva of Human Resources was waiting me outside my room. As I opened the door, I asked her blithely, "What's up?" She matter-of-factly answered, "The company is terminating your contract." I was stunned! Stuttering a bit, she said that I would need to leave the boat before it left the dock. Completely shocked because I'd recently asked management how I was doing and they'd said they'd heard positive things about me, I asked, "Why am I being let go?" Eva mumbled that Joe, the First Cook, was supposed to have told me why. Yes, Joe, the guy I trained to be First Cook, would be taking my job. Captain Mark hadn't planned for Joe to work as a First Cook at all. In fact, he had boldfaced arranged for me to train Joe so that Joe could take my job once I'd been terminated. I was devastated. This action was kept highly under wraps. Even Captain Bob, my BFF, had no idea it was going to happen.

The reason I was given for being let go was ridiculous and clearly fabricated. The official report said, "there had been food complaints." What? I know this reasoning was completely unjustified because when I was fired, many people complained about the fact I was let go and vouched for me as a valuable employee and good cook. As a matter of fact, my entire staff felt so strongly about it that they walked out with me. When I'd asked for a signed copy of the complaints, Eva said she hadn't just listened to idle gossip, that she had proof. But when I insisted that she provide me with any kind of documentation as proof of my "faulty performance," she denied having any names or documents to back her claim. She finally relinquished and gave me one name: Forman Brian Coyne. But when I asked him about it, he said that he had heard rumors of complaints but nothing specific. Then, after telling me I was being let go due to complaints about the food, Eva recanted and said the complaints weren't just about the food, that there was more involved but that she wasn't authorized to discuss it with me anymore. It was all a setup based on nothing.

Personally, one of the many reasons I believe I was let go was due to a time when I was informed, not asked, that I would be going to Russia and if I didn't go, I would be penalized for not finishing my contract. I was ordered to get a passport and an AIDS blood test. The boat would have been in Russia for 65-75 days, far longer than my contract required. I would have no way of getting off and I very much wanted to go home and spend time with my family. I was tired. Plus, protection for women aboard in foreign waters was notably sketchy. It was a fight I didn't want to fight. Another time, I'd reported Captain Mark to the company's head office for sexual harassment. Though it is my assumption this report was confidential, I had made it when a lawyer came to the *Claymore Sea* to consult with me about an unrelated report of sexual harassment that she'd been hearing from other women aboard the *Saga Sea*. While on the subject, I mentioned my own challenges regarding Captain Mark on the *Claymore Sea*. The lawyer then asked me several times if I was satisfied with the way the company handled reports of harassment. I told her I was okay since, by that time, I wasn't working with Captain Mark anymore. Many years later, I found out that the real reason I'd been fired was because the men aboard the vessel were threatened by me. They weren't used to a woman who would fight to keep her job and stand up to men who challenged her.

Fifteen years later, I happened to see Eva at a funeral, the woman who delivered the news of my termination to me and had worked in Human Resources during that time. A new employee, she'd been among those who had fired me from the *Claymore Sea* and had delivered the doleful news of my termination. She told me that I'd lost the position over nothing other than personal agendas of those aboard. She said that she was ashamed at her part in my termination, but she said she'd been admonished if she wanted to keep her job, she should "shut up and do as she was told." She knew Captain Mark's reasons for my termination were fabricated. But like so many others aboard, she was afraid he would retaliate and be vindictive if she didn't follow his strict orders, however unfair they were.

A guy named Greg Shuey was also instrumental in getting me fired. Years after, when I saw him at Dutch Harbor Airport, I ignored him. More recently, I saw him at an industry function. Shabby and wizened, he looked like he'd been living under a bridge. He'd reached out and grabbed my arm. As he did that and subsequently began to talk to me, I thought to myself how amazing it was that some people remember history differently and rewrite it suit their own consciences. It appeared that Greg had done this regarding my termination from the *Claymore Sea*. "Look how far you've come in all your accomplishments," he'd gushed. He said how "proud he was of me" as though he'd had something significant to do with my accomplishments. At one time, he'd sent a food representative to the boat to take back shrimp I'd ordered just to harass me, saying he "thought I was spending too much money." He's only made my job harder and more stressful. Surprised that he'd have the nerve to even talk to me after initiating my dismissal, I looked pointedly at him and replied with emphasis, "I now work for a great company that treats their people well." American Seafoods is and has been a great company to work for. No love lost there – and look who is still working in the industry: me.

By the time I finished working aboard the *Claymore Sea* and weathered the termination drama, I was so emotionally rung out and physically exhausted that I'd decided to "get my land legs," and go back to school for a college degree. I wanted a career change. The *Claymore Sea* had worn me out. However, the minute I'd enrolled in school in July of 1999 and was ready to start, I received a phone call from Roger that changed my course completely. He said he had a friend who'd contacted him with the news that a new company was being established, IMMI. They were looking for a Chief Steward. Apparently, I'd been recommended take the position. Just starting out, the company had a fleet of five boats, all named "Ann," including the *Christina Ann*. They'd been in operation for a few years. IMMI would later sell to American Seafoods (ASC).

Throughout the years I made many themed cakes for the holidays! Valentine's Day cakes, *Claymore Sea.*

Unjust departure and a better future. Farewell, *Claymore Sea.*

Plane leaving Dutch Harbor with Mount Ballyhoo in the background. If you can see the mountain, planes can land.

A couple of our boats in City Dock, Dutch Harbor, Alaska.

SECTION THREE:
ABOARD THE *CHRISTINA ANN,*
KATIE ANN, NORTHERN HAWK,
AND *DYNASTY,* AND
COOKING PORTSIDE

AMERICAN SEAFOODS

CHIEF STEWARD, RELIEF STEWARD, AND FLEET GALLEY ADVISOR

1996 - PRESENT

The *Christina Ann* -
Sisters and Brothers of the Sea

The *Christina Ann* had previously been the Aleutian Speedwell and had been one of the first trawlers in the Bering Sea, so she had a long history of use. When it was offered to me, I chose to accept the position of Chief Steward aboard the *Christina Ann*. This time, the decision would overall prove to be a good one.

From the moment I met Captain John Symzack of the *Christina Ann*, we hit it off right out-the-gate and became great friends. A handsome, recovering drug-addict/alcoholic, Captain John tended to slide from his convictions and binge, which made me sad for him, but he had a good heart and I enjoyed working with him. I took great delight in the banter he created between us. I had begun calling the women crew aboard "Sisters of the Sea." He bantered back to me that the men aboard were "Brothers of the Sea." As the "SOS," I had great fun passing cryptic notes back and forth with Captain John, the "BOS. We'd pass notes all day long under our cabin doors. A friendly rivalry ensued, all in good fun. Recently I found some of these notes. Their banter made me smile with a hint of nostalgia. I remember when these were passed surreptitiously under our respective cabin doors.

Captain John: "As a meaningless and pathetic attempt to infiltrate the BOS, the SOS has failed once again! The brotherhood will not give into the SOS's demands to be noticed and taken seriously as an organized group! The BOS will unite and continue our fight for our long upholding rights-of-passage that you so dearly seek. Any and all attempts to try to compromise these rights will be met with swift and concise measures."

Me: "As SOS, we shall unite and overcome the oppressive, hollow, empty BOS. Though we may be few in numbers, we are an army in strength! We shall persevere for all SOS in the fleet!!!!!!!! And, may our shining example of sisterhood set the standard of the way it will become!!!"

Captain John: "The SOS is just a meaningless, leftist, and somewhat feminist plot to try and overthrow BOS. The Brothers of the Sea will not tolerate any of the SOS's attempts to try and overthrow us. The SOS's ceremoniously pathetic claim to victory is nothing but a plot to try and mentally compromise the BOS's newest member of the brotherhood. Our victory remains untainted! Our rite of passage remains intact! The SOS remains an apparition. We will unite and fight for the rights you so dearly seek!"

Me: "The SOS are everywhere…we are powerful…we live in cyberspace… you cannot knock us down! As each day passes, we grow stronger like a snowball rolling downhill picking up momentum!!!!!!!!! You can delete us, but we will return!!!! Ours is not a "claim" to victory… it is an announcement declaring the sensitive, caring and giving SOS as the winners of this pathetic BOS claim. We will rise to the occasion in unity and strength beyond anything BOS could imagine because we are woman…hear us roar! And, watch us soar, right over your pathetic, hollow lives. You will not succeed in wooing us away from our intent with your flowers and claims to bigger-than-life parts…we will keep you at arm's length until which time that we deem you useful to our needs…about once a month…remember that behind every BOS is a good SOS."

However, for all her wonderful camaraderie among crew, the *Christina Ann* was not noted for being a comfortable boat. She was like a cork in the water and very scary. Top heavy, waves would heave her from side to side, rolling her so violently that water would sweep across her foredeck. Also, my cabin, which I had to share, was so small that its two berths covered the entire space. I couldn't get dressed without banging my hips and shoulders into the bulkheads. I was always bruised from head to foot and cramped for space.

And, if it was even possible, the *Christina Ann's* galley was an even worse one than the galley on the *Claymore Sea*. It was half the size of the *Claymore Sea* galley. One day as I was preparing a dinner of Swedish meatballs in the galley, a storm hit the boat broadside. I was thrown suddenly and forcefully against a stack of hot pots and pans. In a muck of sauce, my meatballs went flying off the stove, flinging through the air, covering me and the galley in a stewed mess. To say this was a commonplace event would be an understatement. A week didn't go by that I wasn't sloshed with something slimy perpetrated by a sudden storm. That time, it took me three days to clean up the debris in the galley.

I would also learn soon that sailors aboard were a rough and tumble crew and would do anything to get a buzz on. I even had to watch to be sure they didn't buy Scope mouthwash while ashore because due to its trace alcohol, these guys would buy it to get high. Pure vanilla is also 30% alcohol. I couldn't use either of these on the boat for the same reason. But the Captain was much more pleasant, and this made working on the *Christina Ann* a far better experience than my nightmare at the *Claymore Sea*.

When I wasn't being doused in food slop and thrown around my cabin during storms, life aboard the *Christina Ann* was very enjoyable and even-keel. I also had a lot of latitude to be creative in my cooking and the crew and staff were good to me. The only problem I had with this boat was my familiar spin with sexual harassment followed me. In this case, the chief engineer on this boat took a liking to me. He would show up in the galley all the time and hang out. He was always flirting with me, but I was so naïve, I didn't realize it. He was a terrible alcoholic and drank on board, which was scary to me. He was the chief engineer! He could have sunk the boat! He used to harass me on a regular basis because he had the hots for me, but I didn't reciprocate. One time, while I was at home in Seattle onshore, he showed up uninvited at my door with a gift. How he got my address is a mystery to me to this day.

But I also made wonderful friends with men aboard who didn't harass me. One deck hand, Randall Lee, who is a great friend of mine to this day, took a liking to an observer on board. Today, the observers are much more trained and rigorous on their jobs and no longer fraternize with crew. In fact, they're not allowed to interact with them. But back then it was different. We were friends with them, and as in Randall's case, sometimes even more. One day, Randall even gave me a day off and came into my galley and he and Kaari (the observer) cooked for me. We also made "mocktails" from extracts

– peppermint schnapps, vanilla, and whatever we could find. We had a lot of fun making them. To this day, Randall thinks he has a hole in his stomach from those drinks. A few years later Randall and Kaari got married.

Additionally, a galley assistant got involved with someone on the boat. Right before dinner she would go and wake him up and they'd fool around. The lights would be off. Like I said, fraternizing was not as frowned on back then as it is today. But it was still done a bit in stealth. As I mentioned, the bunks on the *Christina Ann* were very tiny. This guy had a roommate who slept on the bottom bunk. And, in those days, many of us, including this woman, wore baseball caps because we had long hair. So, she'd grabbed what she thought was her baseball cap and had raced down to the galley because she was late to help me get the meal out. The minute I saw her, I realized she'd dressed in the dark because rather than her usual baseball cap, she had her guy's roommate's nasty, smelly fish hat on her head. It reeked so strongly of the stench that I felt nauseous. But I winked at her none-the-less and said, "Ran late and got dressed in the dark this morning, did you?" She fingered the hat and let out a shriek. We both laughed out loud. Nobody said a word to her about that smelly, tattered hat as we served them their food. From that point on, she was more careful. But our comradery was sealed. Women crew had to stick together and support each other aboard. It kept us sane.

Three poignant moments that so clearly illustrated to me how lonely being out on the water can be and how estranged you are from your everyday life and the people you love ashore also happened on the *Christina Ann.*

One of my galley assistants, Trish Berry, had a husband who had worked on the boat and he'd convinced me to hire her. He'd subsequently developed cancer and had become too ill to work. He was at home failing rapidly, and we kept trying to get her off the boat. However, rough weather, pounding waves and high winds made it impossible for us to skiff her to shore. The weather was so bad. I'll never forget how she'd stand looking out the bridge windows watching and waiting for the weather to come down, wishing so desperately that she could get home to be with her husband before he passed. It was heartbreaking to watch. We did manage to get her home before he passed, which was a blessing, but that waiting time on the boat was excruciatingly painful for her. Trish went on to work with me on a couple more boats.

The captain was also in ill health, slowly was dying from the "demons of drugs and alcohol," no doubt partially due to his family dysfunction. One time he was called off the boat because his mother's boyfriend had murdered her. We were able to get him off the boat, but again, the waiting was also very difficult for him.

Perhaps the most painful time suffered by someone else that I remember regarding being away from family was when a guy named Andy received the news his brother had died. We were out to sea and, again, the weather was too rough to skiff him off the boat. So, he had to wait for days before he could go home. Though a full-grown man with strength to spare, the poor guy spent the entire time he waited curled up on his bunk, weeping non-stop. To be so far away from family at such a truncating time was a miserable, inevitable side-effect of our fishing life.

I had a similar experience in my own life. While working on the *Christina Ann*, my father passed away. Luckily, I was at home when it happened. However, I had to go back to work shortly after this event. Fortunately for me, my ex-sister-in-law was aboard, so at least I had the benefit of having someone near me who'd known and loved my dad. She hugged and consoled me as I cried for an entire month. I will never forget her compassion.

At this point in your reading of this book, you may think everyone aboard but me was an alcoholic, carousing maniac, but that wasn't true. Many of crew just quietly did their jobs. They were there to achieve a goal of making enough money to pursue other lifetime dreams. One couple was working aboard so they could buy a house. Others worked to keep abreast of a desired lifestyle. While some, like me, wanted to later pay for school and propel themselves into a different tax bracket and finer lifestyle. This quote I found attached to an old binder pretty much sums up how I was feeling at the time. Attitude, more than anything, was a key to survival.

"I love the work dynamics here. It's incomparable because people go through their emotional roller coasters and don't apologize. That's what gets me. I mean, it's raw human behavior

at times and it makes me giggle because it's not something I'm used to. It gets weird and primal out here. I need to check myself and ask WTF? But we're all governed by different rules at sea and each of us work within our parameters. Every morning, I'm mentally prepared for the task at hand and know myself well enough to keep my head up and my head in the game. It's interesting how the dynamics play out at the end of the day. I don't forget to enjoy the scenery and the idiosyncrasies that become fodder for anecdotes to family and friends. I've got dinner, ice cream, and a fantastic novel awaiting me in my cabin before I put this day into my back pocket."

The galley of the *Christina Ann* was so small that my office was in the pantry! In this photo, John Winslett, bosun, is assisting me.

Randal Lee, Rakal, and Judy in front of the Elbowroom, *Christina Ann*.

Crew in the mess on the *Christina Ann*.

Small galley on the *Christina Ann.*

Randal Lee (Deckhand) helping barbecue...flipping burgers, *Christina Ann.*

Deck crew on the *Christina Ann*, 1997.

Sindi, Trish, and halibut.

Eating ice cream cones with the deck crew on the *Christina Ann.*

Randal Lee and "Mocktails," *Christina Ann.*

Rakal (Rachael), my First Cook, on the *Christina Ann*.

(Caption)

/ Underground gun turret left over from World War II, Unalaska. /

Aboard the *Katie Ann* –
January 1999 - March 2001

In January of 1999, American Seafood Company (ASC) acquired all the "Ann" boats and kept only one in service. I was also the only steward they chose to rehire from another boat when they repurposed that vessel and named it *Katie Ann*. Though only retaining one boat, ASC was able to keep all the other "Ann" vessels' fishing quotas combined. This strategy authorized the *Katie Ann* to pull in a much larger yield of fish. As a result, my pay was going to be very good.

Assigned to this new vessel headed through the Pacific Northwest to Dutch Harbor, I couldn't help but notice that the *Katie Ann* was aged, lengthy and very dirty. Once aboard, the days were also long and the weather often inhospitable.

Our captain's name was Jim, but we all called him Skippy. A brisk, no-nonsense guy, we loved teasing him. One day I raced up to the wheelhouse in a panic.

"Skippy!" I yelled, "Come quickly! My galley assistant, Trish, has gashed her finger! She's cut the tip of her finger clean off and it's bleeding horribly!"

Skippy looked dutifully alarmed. Panicked, he raced after me to the galley. Trish was there with her hand wrapped in what looked like a bloody mess. We'd really made fake blood out of corn syrup and red food coloring to tease Skippy. He was so mad at us! I watched my back for a long while after that!

On February 5, 1999, I got the news that my Aunt Rose had passed away. She was like a second mom to me as I grew up with her and my cousins.

It wasn't unexpected but it knocked the wind out of me, nonetheless. My cousins told me they would wait for me to come home to hold her memorial. It was only one of two times in my fishing history that a boat had a "stand down," which meant everyone voluntarily tied to the dock for a week. So, it was a perfect timing for me to go home.

But getting back to the *Katie Ann* was an adventure in and of itself. The boat had already departed from Dutch Harbor for the fishing grounds when I returned. So, to get back to the *Katie Ann*, I had to take a little "longliner," or fishing boat that uses long lines, otherwise known as a catcher boat. The Muirmuach was filthy and the captain, Dave, was quirky. He wore port and starboard high-top tennis shoes; one green shoe on his right foot (starboard) and one red one on his left foot (port). Since there wasn't a bunk for me, I had to sleep in the wheelhouse in a tiny, dirty day bed and listen to the dead man alarm go off all night to keep the person on watch awake. It was rugged. The little boat also pitched and rolled around so much that I felt a bit seasick. We went on the hunt looking for the *Katie Ann*, to no avail. We went to King Cove...not there. Then to Cold Bay...not there either. We traversed back and forth, while the crew fished in between our search. After a week of bouncing around in the Bering Sea, that little piss pot of a boat began to wear on my last nerve. Since I was a cook, the expectation was that I would cook for my passage fare. I did not feel well, so I ended up doing very little cooking. Finally, much to my dismay after all that bouncing, pitching, rolling, and seasick nausea, we ended up going back to where we had started – Dutch Harbor. The *Katie Ann* looked like a cruise boat in comparison after corking around on that little boat! All that, and the captain would not release me to go back to the *Katie Ann* until I had cooked his entire crew a full breakfast. It had been a sobering time for me, with much time for reflection.

Katie Ann was a hard boat but working there would ultimately change my life forever. I'd met the factory manager, John, and sensed he had interest in me. But I wasn't sure how I felt about him and, moreover, didn't want to jeopardize my job by getting involved with him. We'd had nice chats, one of them even in his room, but I was being very cautious. When Dewy, a guy I'd been interested in, came aboard and gave me a big hug, I felt John's jealousy and wasn't sure what to think about it. Dewy told me he had a "sort of girlfriend," though, and broke my heart, leaving an opening for John to come in.

When Rick Black, our observer, saw John around me, he predicted John and I would get married someday. I remember laughing at the notion. He teased me daily about it. John was a good-looking, lanky man with an easy-going manner, long stride and great smile, but he wasn't my type at all. Or, so I thought at the time. We shared an office, though, and as we began to get to know each other, my perspective about him started to change. I liked him.

On Monday, January 30th, 2000, John asked me if he could kiss me. I said no because he had a cold. He asked me if he could when his cold was gone. That Thursday he said he said that he really liked me and would never hurt me. He changed his hours so he could be on the same shift as mine. On Saturday, February 2nd, 2000, his cold was gone, and he kissed me. Then, I really started to like him. One thing led to another and despite my apprehension about diving right in and uncertainty about whether I would get too attached, too fast and too soon, we became involved. He told me he was falling in love with me. Exactly 21 days after our first kiss, on February 23rd, 2000, we spent our first night together. It was wonderful and exciting. As he gently kissed me deeply and wrapped me in his arms, I felt blissfully happy, safe and warm. And, just like that, I was smitten.

Once John and I got closer, it was against the rules, a real "no-no" for us to fool around. We could have both lost our jobs if we'd been found out. So, we had to be very careful of the alone time we spent together. One night I went to John's room to watch a movie. As we cuddled up together, we heard a sudden knock on John's cabin door. Captain Skippy called out to John. As the door opened, I slipped behind it to hide. Mind you, John was a factory manager, which meant he worked in the operations section of the vessel all day slicing fish heads and dissecting fish innards. His coveralls, all of which were hanging on the door, were slimy and smelly. I had my face pressed up against them, trying not to gag as I breathed in their pungency. The things a gal does for love!

I will never forget what happened a few days later. I was down in the dry stores on a ladder and Trish, who was the only person aboard who knew of my interest in John, ran up to me, ashen faced, yelling, "Sindi! John's been hurt and its very serious! Don't do anything. Stay right here. I'll let you know what's going on but it's not good." I had brought Trish over to the *Katie Ann* from the *Christina Ann* and trusted her implicitly. She was like my daughter. But since my relationship with John was unknown to anyone but her, I had a long wait wondering what had happened and what the outcome might be." I thought, "Oh my god. I've only just started dating this guy." Death came easy at sea on the fishing vessels and I knew John was around a lot of heavy equipment that was designed to cut through large quantities of fish. The waiting was excruciating.

When I was finally able to see him in the skin room (where the crew changed into rubberized overalls to work in the factory), much to my alarm, he was sitting on the deck on a bench holding what was left of his arm. His entire arm was dripping on to the floor. How the man didn't cut a major artery is a miracle. It was the most damaging wound I've ever seen before or since. I will never forget how calm and stalwart he was in the middle of what had to be horrific pain. One of the previous mates, John Szymzack, had apparently been a user, and cleaned out what was left of the pain meds aboard. So, John was experiencing near loss of his arm with no pain killers at all. It was unbelievable but John told me he wasn't feeling any pain. He said that he had reached down to pick up a fish from the deck and the fish processor, the BAADER (header), had grabbed his rain gear and filleted his arm at the elbow three times before they could stop the machine. His arm was hanging by mere threads. Bone and nerves were exposed. It's a wonder his arm didn't fall right off, but he was holding on to it and keeping it attached by its bleeding tendons. We had to irrigate his arm every couple of hours to keep it moist. We had a highly trained EMT aboard, Shawn Brent, and John and I both believe Shawn saved his arm. He was a very experienced EMT who worked on our boat as a factory tech. He wasn't a doctor, but he knew his stuff.

We managed to get John to the officer's mess hall and made a sling out of cardboard. In the middle of all that pain, his main concern was who was going to do his job and how bad he felt for the crew because production had been forced to stop because of his accident. I believe watching him at that moment face so much pain and risk with such calm resolve is the moment I realized I was in love with him. He had to wait in pain, too, until we reached

Adak, Alaska. As I continued to work and help him medically at the same time, I had to concentrate very hard on not showing how deeply I cared about John to others. It was hard to not show the deep emotion I had during that event. I was torn up inside worrying about him.

It took eighteen hours for us to steam to Adak, on Adak Island in the western Aleutian Islands in Alaska. With a population of only 316 people in 2000, it was sparsely populated. But there was a small airport in town. Before giving the island back to the Native Alaskans, the navy had owned Adak. So, it had a very good runway. We'd hoped to have John air-lifted by Lear Jet from Adak. But the weather was too fierce, and the plane headed for John from Anchorage had to turn around. American Seafoods Company then diverted a c-130 to Adak. A turboprop military transport aircraft designed as a medevac and cargo transport aircraft, the c-130 can fly through anything and land anywhere. Amazingly, while waiting for the c-130 to arrive, John was able to walk off the *Katie Ann* with assistance to the clinic on Adak, holding the remains of his arm. He stayed there for many hours.

"Can't you tell me anything about how he's doing?" I wanted to wail to Captain Skippy. But I couldn't be obvious in my affection and concern. I had to be discrete about asking for too much information about John once he left the boat for the clinic to protect both of our jobs.

As it usually does in Adak, the weather was blowing wildly. Winter squalls can bring wind gusts of over 120 miles per hour to that area. In fact, when the wind blows in Adak, the wind is so violent that the town center blasts loud sirens like bomb shelter sirens to warm people to stay inside. Due to this inhospitable weather, we were stuck on the dock. We could do nothing but wait, and wait, and wait.

After what seemed a lifetime, in six to eight hours, the c-130 finally landed in Adak and took John to the hospital in Anchorage. By that time, John had nearly gone into full-blown shock.

At the time, I knew very little about John and even less about his family. So, I emailed my friend who was a purser on another boat at the time. As a purser, she had access to all medical information and gave me the phone number of the hospital. I was able to go to the ship's phone and talk to John right before they took him into surgery. To be able to do that back in those days was incredible.

"I'm headed into surgery. They're going to do all they can to save my arm," he assured me.

John's brother, Dave, was John's emergency contact. When they called him, his comment was, "Do everything you can to save that man's arm." Miraculously, they did just that – John's arm was saved, to later heal completely.

John and I developed a great relationship through writing countless long emails to each other. Talking by phone was difficult since cell phones were practically non-existent at the time. Nobody knew about my relationship with him - we wrote emails in secret. Our love for each other grew stronger.

Though John went home to Seattle, I stayed on the *Katie Ann* for over a month. John was in physical therapy by the time I got home. I told him that I would have stayed with him even if he had lost his arm. Later I would jokingly tell him, "I'm glad you kept your arm because when I told you I would stay with you if you lost it, I was just trying to be nice. I didn't mean a word of what I said!" Truly, I wasn't that invested in the relationship at that point. We had only just begun our relationship. We were only a few weeks into our relationship at that point. But as it turned out, Rick Black's prediction came true. On November 2, 2003, surrounded by our children, family, and fishing friends, John and I exchanged our vows. We've been happily married ever since.

Food prep (shrimp skewers) in the galley, *Katie Ann*.

Katie Ann Chief Engineer Steve Kostbow demonstrates his carrot peeling skill.

Katie Ann Chief Engineer Steve
Kostbow didn't like the smell of the
lamb I cooked that day.

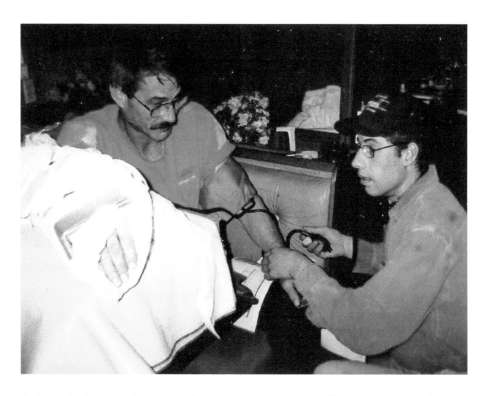

On the *Katie Ann* when John nearly lost his arm at the elbow. EMT Shawn Brent saved John's arm.

EMT Shawn Brent saved John's arm.

Foreman Terry Sutton (RIP) was very supportive in helping me learn "the ropes of commercial fishing."

First Cook, Tim Wetherill, and
Terry (RIP).

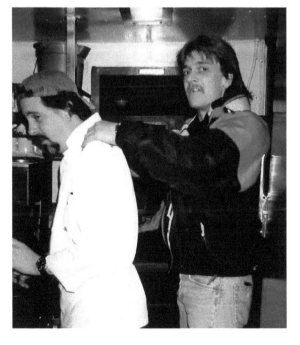

Captain John Szymzak (RIP), *Katie Ann*. Top photo and bottom photo.

Tim Wetherill (1st Cook),
Katie Ann.

Jim McDonald,
("Jimmy 4-Trip"), our
food representative from
Charlie's Produce. I have
known him since he
was 18 years old.

Captain Mark, nicknamed Skippy, *Katie Ann* (B Season). We made him bread slippers.

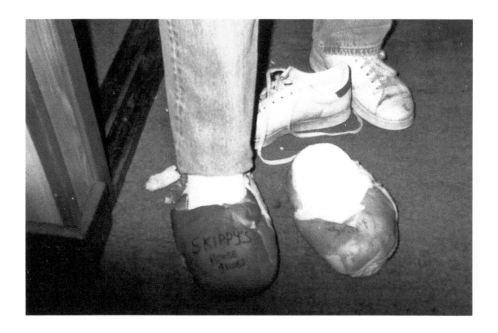

Captain Skippy's bread slippers (close-up), *Katie Ann*.

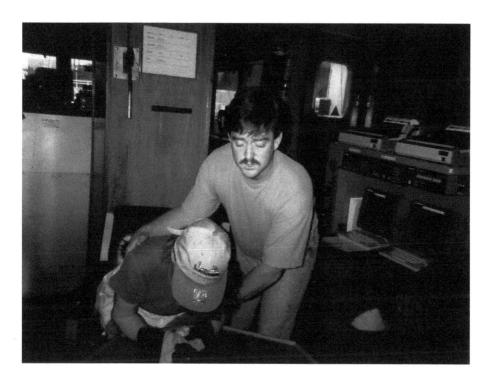

Captain Skippy comforting Trish with a fake cut finger, *Katie Ann.*

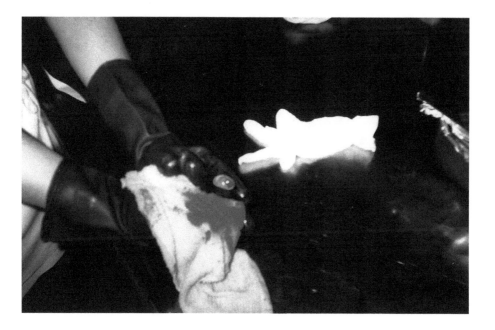

Playing a joke on Captain Skippy of the *Katie Ann*, Trish pretended to sever her finger.

We come in all sizes! Trish, me, and Mohammed, *Katie Ann.*

Roger Mjeltevik's daughter, Monet, came to visit her Lou-Lou, *Katie Ann.*

The "Man Basket." This is how we transferred people.

Tiny galley to work in on the *Katie Ann*.

Sandwiches on homemade bread on the *Katie Ann*.

These are large steam kettles.

The *Katie Ann* in Dutch Harbor, Alaska.

Kjetil Saatre the best "Fishmaster" in the fleet. This macrame (a knot tying) boat was made by him. He has made many of these 3D and flat boats.

/ Northern Hawk /

Aboard the *Northern Hawk* – 2001 – 2007

My tenure on the *Katie Ann* ended in April of 2000 when the *Northern Hawk* needed a Chief Steward. I jumped at the opportunity to work on a bigger boat with a better equipped galley. Little did I know that the six-year drama on this boat was also going to be much bigger! When I began the job, I had no idea that it would be the hardest I would ever work physically on a boat, not to mention I'd once again be back under the scrutiny of a critical, over-bearing, condescending captain. We inherited a crew who had been with the *Northern Hawk* for thirty years. The captain, whose name will go unmentioned for litigious reasons, was one of them. For the next six years, his manner with me would leave me feeling diminished and demoralized. The sad fact is, he had no idea how badly his behavior toward the crew was affecting all of us. In particular, he was clueless about his misogyny.

But as I stepped aboard the *Northern Hawk* in Seattle, it was a swelteringly hot day in July 2001. Sweat poured down my back and my soggy shirt clung to me. I'd never been on this boat, so everything about it was new. Looking at her sleek lines, I faced her 410 feet stretched out elegantly on the dock with anticipation and excitement. She was a beautiful boat. I guessed that her galley would be filled with wonderful equipment for cooking up fabulous Swedish meatball stews and hearty fried chicken. To my dismay, my reverie was short. I discovered that I'd been immediately assigned the daunting duty of backloading the previous steward's food supply, which meant hauling it single-handedly from the dock to the boat.

After backloading 28 pallets of food for the 120 to 130 crew members aboard, I was exhausted. I had no idea where I was supposed to store anything. I'd had no introduction to any procedures or anyone, for that matter. Though I had no idea where anything went or what I was supposed to do, I was still expected to prepare crew meals immediately. Then, after backloading for 13-14 hours, I was subjected to my new captain's infamous, frequently held two-hour safety meeting, held on the bow of the boat in the sweltering heat. I would soon learn that whether our trip began with intolerable heat, frigid snowstorms or on the blustery dock in Dutch Harbor, every trip included a tedious, lengthy safety meeting identical to this one. The Captain loved to hear himself talk and would drone on and on in long-winded speeches, no matter where we were. Though I appreciated his adherence to safety, these meetings were excruciatingly long. After many complaints over the years, they were finally slightly shortened. All crew breathed a collective sigh of relief.

But standing in that disorganized galley, I heard my voice called loudly over the boat's speaker. "Sindi Giancoli, come to the Bridge." The Captain's booming voice echoed throughout the vessel. Little did I know then that over the years, I'd become so belittled and criticized by him about my cooking and my ability to make sound judgments as a manager of housekeeping and the galley, that when I'd hear that call from the bridge, I'd feel sick to my stomach and start to cry. I knew the only reason I'd be summoned was to be scolded about something completely unfair.

(In this book, I refer to him only as "The Captain" because I suspect if I used his real name, he's just the type to sue me for defamation of character. In fact, he told me that he would!)

One such scolding involved him querying me as to why I'd hired two housekeepers. This was a 410-foot vessel, so two housekeepers for that size boat and its 130 crew did not seem excessive. The prior season, he pointed out, did just fine with only one housekeeper. In his opinion, the boat had been cleaner before. I disagreed with him. I'd also had to let one of our previous housekeepers go because of multiple crew complaints. She just wasn't working out. He told me that I had not documented her no-rehire to his satisfaction. He also said that my actions made him look bad because the housekeeper I'd let go was hired by American Seafood Company to work on another boat. Then he complained that the housekeepers I did hire were not painting the fan room or decks, which needed new paint jobs. Though it was not their job to do this, he said they should be taking that initiative. Or, that I should do the painting job. As if I didn't have enough to do feeding 130 people twice a day! He also asked about having the deck four rooms cleaned. I said that he was the only person on deck four that wanted a room cleaning and that none of the other crew minded cleaning their own rooms. He told me I was lying. In the "old days," housekeeping cleaned some of the officer's rooms, but that practice was not done much anymore. Captains work twelve hours a day and make much more money than others who work countless more hours and make far less money. They should be able to clean their own cabins. I tried to tell him that with as many crew members as were aboard, far more than before, more work needed to be done. With two housekeepers, laundry would not get backed up and the heads and change room would be cleaned twice daily. He deemed that unnecessary. Of course, when the factory started up and the change rooms did not get cleaned in a timely way, he went down to the change room when the crew was on a break and asked them if there were any concerns. It was no surprise to me that they said the change room needed cleaning. I was criticized for it being dirty. I felt he fabricated problems with the sole purpose of criticizing me.

Another time, he insisted that he wanted me to cook food to accommodate his diet. He did not want carbohydrates or foods, like desserts, that contained fat. When I complied, he complained that I did not feed him deep-fried fish. However, he would not allow me to draw up a menu for him to help choose what he wanted to eat. He was impossible to please. I decided to stay out of his way as much as possible. Over the six years I worked on the *Northern Hawk*, I felt that he held me accountable for every move I made on the boat. He had a propensity for turning small issues, like the housekeeping one, into major storms.

He also refused to help people make phone calls. "I could have a catastrophic failure," he'd say. "I'm not a phone operator." In those days, if we wanted to make a ship-to-shore call, we needed to do it through the bridge. He refused to help anyone. When we were out to sea, contact with home was imperative. It kept us steady and sane.

The Captain intimidated people and thought everyone liked him. And, initially, there had been a time during which we'd experienced a good rapport. We had talked about his kids. He came to Leavenworth to our cabin with his family and all was great. But he was different on the boat. The phone would ring in the galley from the wheelhouse and I'm not kidding you, my stomach would tighten I would start to cry because I knew he was going to summon me to the bridge and chew me out about something. Really, it was horrible. I kept hoping when I bound up to the Bridge that he would have good news for me. But that was never true, even one day when, in an upbeat mood, I'd decided to share some good news with him about a recent menu that had been very well received by crew. Before I could blurt out the good news, I was met immediately with criticism of my work. Out of all my years of fishing, working on the *Northern Hawk* was probably the hardest work I'd ever done during the time I had to work with him. There were two other guys who would later work on the *Northern Hawk* that made it easier for me. But while working with "The Captain," life aboard the *Northern Hawk* was terrible and stressful. It's not as though he harassed me in any sexual way. He just beat me down in very condescending and demeaning ways and made me feel inadequate all the time. He would compare me to my relief, Terri, and ask, "how come you can't be more like Terri?" I would answer with frustration. "I'm not Terri. I work differently. I don't want to be compared to her."

Our safety manager, Suzy, had attended the same maritime academy as our captain, so you would have thought that he would have not only been pleased to have her aboard but also hold her in higher regard. She was fearless, talented, strong, and a gifted safety manager. She is, and always will be my SOS (Sister of the Sea). I admired Suzy's accomplishments greatly. She subsequently moved on from the *Northern Hawk* but is still involved in the fishing industry. Unfortunately, the Captain's misogynistic personality was stronger than his respect for her. For a short while, he puffed around talking about how they'd gone to the same academy, but in the end, he was very condescending to her and cut her off at the knees whenever he could. We bonded because we were both strong females in supervisory roles - and so we had each other's backs.

Fishmaster is the name given to the Norwegians - Kjetil Saetre, our Fishmaster, and Kjell, who sailed as our First Mate, also made my life on the

Northern Hawk bearable. Kjetil was the best fishmaster in the fleet and a master at catching fish. When either of them was on watch, I'd join them on the Bridge after my shift was done. Long conversations into the night would follow. Kjetil and I found out were going to be first-time grandparents at the same time. I still only have one and he has eight.

Other than Roger, who is now the VP of American Seafood Company, the best Chief Engineer I'd ever sailed with was also aboard the *Northern Hawk*. Mike Madsen was from Maine, and during our slack time, we had great times together. As I've said, on a boat, you want the engineer to be your friend! I took this to heart. We are friends to this day.

One day, while waking early on the *Northern Hawk*, I gazed out my porthole and watched the sunrise slowly from the horizon, its light casting a pink, hazy, brilliant glow across the water. Though I'd weathered many harassments, harsh weather, physical challenges, and emotional upheaval on fishing vessels, and particularly on this one, I never tired of looking out my porthole into that beautiful, tranquil seascape. Nothing was quite so serene. But I'd also watch the inevitable environmental impact of our nets and ached inside because of it. As our nets were hauled up from the deck, hundreds upon hundreds of feet of rope, countless different species of fish would drop from the net to the deck. Coral, starfish, piles of garbage, plastic, would pull in from the sea in their webs. I saw pallets floating by and watched soap discharge out the side of our boat into the ocean. There was so much unnecessary waste. I couldn't help but wonder about the impact we were having on the sea and its natural life.

After leaving the *Northern Hawk*, it took me a year to finally muster the courage up to write the captain an email and voice what a devastating impact he'd had on me. At the time, he was on the *Northern Hawk* but working for a different company. By this time, the *Northern Hawk* had sold to a Native American Corporation, or Alaskan natives. American Seafood Company would later negotiate a deal with the corporation to use one of their boats. As a part of that negotiation, the captain, engineers, factory manager, and chief steward were all retained. However, within two years of the sale, all would be relieved of their positions.

I wrote:

Captain,

As you can see, I have been holding on to your email for over a year. I have been waiting to collect my thoughts on how I wanted to respond to you. After seeing you in Dutch, and noticing your behavior toward me, I had to really think about what I wanted to say to you. You've hurt a lot of the females' feelings on The Hawk during the years I worked there. I know you think you're being clever, but your comments are hurtful and degrading. Why you feel the need to constantly belittle me as to my skills as a Chief Steward baffles me. I do not comment on your lack of or capabilities to catch fish or not catch fish. You see, that is not how friends treat one another. The way you talk to me and treat me is really embarrassing, but not only for me. It makes others uncomfortable too. I've heard people say many times, "Why does he say those things to you?" It makes you look like an ass. I am a good person and good cook – people genuinely like and care about me. You have your way of running your ship, but it is fear based and lacking in respect. Your entire crew is afraid of you. Nobody wants to come to the Bridge and "chit-chat" with you. When you speak to people, they jump. The Hawk is the only boat I've worked on in 20 years where that is the case. You remind me of a kid who grew up bullied and now you're the Big Bad Captain and everyone must listen to you when you talk. I would like to call you friend, but you must stop poking me with a stick."

He wrote me back and said,

"Obviously I have been too blind and dumb and oblivious of having hurt your feelings with stupid 'jokes' that I have made about your cooking. That has been incredibly insensitive of me and I humbly apologize."

I pointed out to him that he was the one person I tried to please, to no avail. He argued that Megan, our housekeeper had liked him, to which I also pointed out that when he told her he needed paper towels and she had responded by saying, "I can rectify that," and he'd quipped back at her, "that's a big word for a housekeeper."

He responded that he meant it as a joke, but it wasn't funny to Megan – it felt demeaning to her and it stung. He also said he'd thought that we were close enough friends that he'd felt free making "break your balls" kinds of "jokes" about my cooking. I pointed out that while I had tough skin on the outside, it was a different story inside. He simply had no clue how obnoxious he was. At the time, though, management had received multiple private complaints about him. He was pulled off the boat and received a stern condemnation. Coming back on the boat after talking at the office, he was a different person.

The Captain lived in the same town as me, Woodinville, Washington, so weeks later, we met for coffee to discuss my email and his reaction to it. He was dumbfounded and clueless about how he was impacting others. I told him,

"You know, I think that you just don't know how your personality comes across on the boat."

I knew he had it in him to be different. I'd been to parties and dinners at his house. He'd vacationed at John and my cabin in Leavenworth, Washington. He was a completely different man off the boat. I ended our interaction on a positive note by saying, "Let's try to keep our garden of friendship growing. We may need to fertilize it often and occasionally pull some weeds, but I think we have the basis for a long-standing friendship."

I felt that I was standing up for all women in the fishing industry. His willingness to try to change was one small stride toward a change of attitude. As a result, to this day I consider him a friend.

Barbecuing aboard the *Northern Hawk.*

Barbecuing with Jeff Singer in front of the *Northern Hawk.*

Jared serenades me as I do prep work on the *Northern Hawk*.

Lance, from the office helping out in the galley.

/ Sunsets were amazing on the water.
View of Dutch Harbor. /

Aboard the *Dynasty* – 2007- 2008

Though the *Dynasty* had a great crew and Bridge, there's a joke in the fishing industry that it is a career-ender. Though it wasn't for me, it did come close to being one. This would be the last boat I'd work on full-time out to sea.

I can't say that I was always happy working on the *Northern Hawk*, but I'd built my galley equipment and trained my staff, so everything was running smoothly. Given the elements and conditions in which we had to work, I'd organized the galley and made it not only functional and operational, but also efficient. I had trained staff in both the galley and in housekeeping. Everything was working fine. But, to my complete confusion and dismay, suddenly Roger, our VP, decided that it would be beneficial to the company to "mix it up" and move all the Chief Stewards to other boats. To my way of thinking, it was a bad idea.

There's an old axiom, "if it isn't broken, don't fix it." That was certainly true in this case. Whatever possessed Roger to implement this idea, I will never know. It was a debacle. All of us had to leave our trained crew and galley equipment behind. To recreate what we'd had in our previous galleys, we had to buy new equipment and retrain our inherited crew. This was costly to the company and totally inefficient. The only Chief Steward happy about the rotation was a chief steward who was moved from a small boat to our flagship, the newest, biggest boat in the company. But the rest of us grumbled.

My first day aboard, as I was sorting out my galley and determining what I would need to make it my own, I was startled to see a galley assistant, with whom I'd be working, glibly throwing plastic wrap out the porthole. "What do you think you're doing?" I blurted out loudly. "That is absolutely not okay!" He looked at me expressionless. "But that's what Tim, the former Steward did," he objected. "That's how it's done on our boat." I said, "It's my galley now and you'll need to follow my rules." This did not sit well with him. In the male-dominated fishing industry, I often faced men who bristled when taking instruction from a woman. That I held higher rank than them didn't matter. This guy was finally told by the boat's First Mate that he would have to adhere to what I said. I was this guy's boss.

From that day on, the guy and I did not get along. It was no longer the former steward's galley. It was mine. But he thought he knew everything and that I knew nothing. He fought me at every turn, ignoring my instructions. He persisted in doing everything "the old way," or "his way." When in frustration I finally gave him a less-than-stellar evaluation for this reason, he became belligerent with me. He did not return the following season.

In 2008, I would also decide to change how I worked with the company. After I left the Dynasty, when I decided to give up sailing full time, I set myself up to become the Port/Fleet Steward. The idea I proposed to management was an excellent one and they accepted it. Every season end, someone had to cook in port, and no one really wanted to be selected for that duty. However, we all had to take turns. I proposed that I would sail a trip or two every season, support Operations and galley issues, and cook lunch on one of our vessels during shipyard time in which all repairs are done before the next season. It would become a perfect fit for me. I could still be involved in the fishing industry that was so much a part of my life. Plus, I could go home every night. The sailing time when I was needed typically only lasted a month or two. Eventually, after a few years of occasional sailing, the times I was pressed into at sea service lessened, which was fine by me. By now I'd earned the privilege of sailing and cooking in port on every one of the vessels in our fleet. I do have my favorite boat I like to cook on, too.

Two life-changing events had happened to me that year. First, unhappy results came back from a mammogram. I tested positive for breast cancer. Second, my daughter told me that she was pregnant. I decided these two factors were signals that I should stop going to sea on extended fishing trips.

I asked to work as a portside steward. And, I still sailed a few trips on the boats as a relief steward.

As it turned out, working as a portside relief steward was really the best of both worlds. From 2008 until the present day, I've worked in this way part-time. When the boats are in, I cook for crew. The hardest part of cooking portside is not knowing how many people will show up for lunch. But the benefit is, if I run out of food, I can easily pick up the phone and order more. I am also in charge of training new people and passing my know-how on to a younger generation. Plus, the hardest part of cooking at sea was calculating how much food to buy so that we didn't run out of provisions. On land, calculating provisioning concerns isn't an issue. Working inside a shipyard is also easier on my nerves. It is very different from the emotionally charged environment at sea where I had to respond daily to people's likes and dislikes and social politics. I don't have to weather fractious and difficult personalities or abrasive, emotional outbursts from disgruntled crew. Moreover, at the shipyard, everyone is happy to see me. They are hungry and appreciate having a good meal portside. "People will take a burned cookie from a happy cook" is my mantra.

In 2013, American Seafood made the portside steward position full-time. Since, it's been elevated to the title of "Fleet Galley Advisor," with expanded responsibilities. As such, in addition to portside cooking, I initiate and manage training, support hiring of galley crew, and train people how to prepare budgets and use computers.

There are still times when I am needed aboard to do short runs, but I don't go out anymore unless it's necessary.

Boats in Dutch Harbor, Alaska.

Little Siener in Dutch Harbor, Alaska.

American Dynasty at the Koosterboor dock. This was the last boat I sailed on.

Aerial view of a couple of
American Seafoods boats at the
Kloosterboer dock.

/ Beautiful Prince William Sound /

Prince William Sound

On one occasion, however, I did join a longer trip out of Seattle to Prince William Sound, where I stayed for a month. On a brisk morning in August of 2002, the *Katie Ann* steamed into the stunning waters of Prince Edward Sound in the Gulf of Alaska on the east side of the Kenai Peninsula. It was nothing short of awe-inspiring. Flanked by the snow-capped, craggy Chugach mountain range to the east and north and by a lush green Kenai Peninsula to the west, the Sound covered 3,800 miles of Alaskan coastline. Numerous small islands were located throughout Prince William Sound, including one named Whittier, which was the *Katie Ann's* ultimate destination. This region is vitally important to the fishing industry and is well-known for its wild Alaskan salmon, which is why we were there. The *Katie Ann* would serve as the "mother ship" for tender boats which would bring us salmon for processing. I cooked some of that salmon for the crew aboard the *Katie Ann*.

Prince William Sound's largest port is Valdez, at the southern terminus of the Trans-Alaska Pipeline System. It is so beautiful there, it's hard to imagine that on March 24, 1989 a massive oil spill occurred in its waters, infamously known as the Exxon Valdez oil spill. The oil tanker Exxon Valdez, bound for Long Beach, California, struck Prince William Sound's Bligh Reef just west of Tatitlek, Alaska. Considered to be one of the worth human-caused environmental disasters of all time, the accident spilled 10.8 million U.S. gallons of crude oil into Prince William Sound. The region's remote location, accessible only by helicopter, float planes, or boats, made it difficult for any immediate government or industry response. The spill affected 1,300 miles of coastline. Sea otters, seals, and seabirds in the area suffered greatly.

Resting at the top of the Passage Canal, Whittier is considered the gateway to Prince William Sound. Established as a military supply port in World War II, its mostly used today for fishing and tourism. Wildlife is also now abundant and rigorously protected there. We saw plenty of the wildlife in our off-duty time. Once the tenders had delivered their salmon and we'd processed it, we would climb out of the boat and travel by skiff through the Sound's pristine fjords to the glaciers and pick blueberries. Remote and pristine, the area was breathtaking. As a matter of fact, it was so breathtaking that some people after leaving the boat overstayed their visit. On one such occasion, my galley assistant, Trish, and a first engineer, Cliff, took a skiff out to one of the islands in Prince William Sound. The tide went out and they were stuck on a glacier. As peaceful and serene as the glaciers were, Trish and Cliff experienced a moment of sharp alarm when they realized they were stranded. Though global warming is taking its toll on Alaskan glaciers in recent times, back then they were still quite massive. Being stranded on one was a sobering experience. Luckily, Trish and Cliff were reported missing, a search party went out, and they were located and brought back to the boat no worse for wear.

For as peaceful an experience as Whittier, Alaska could be, the experience was also not without its heart-in-your-throat thrilling moments for me.

I'd flown up to Prince Edward Sound on a rickety, two-seater float plane. Sensing my nervousness, the pilot made me fly the plane. We saw pristine ice-blue glaciers and long horned sheep grazing in the mountains below us. It was a beautiful flight. The spans were so stunning I forgot my apprehension. As we landed in the water, the impact caused huge wakes to spray against the sides of the plane. I'd yelped in surprise. But that wasn't the only surprise on that trip. Getting home was even more exhilarating.

To get home, I needed to go on the tender boat from Artic Harbor to reach the small army base of Whittier. There, I would be transported through a tunnel which only has car access during part of the day, with the remainder of the day closed for train use. If you don't get there before 10:00 A.M., you can't get through it. It's the longest tunnel in the Northern Hemisphere, 3 ½ miles long. It was my ticket out to Anchorage and my flight home. The tiny tender boat which I rode to Whittier was, in fact, quite pleasant, with a hot tub in the back of the boat. But the day I was scheduled to connect with a flight out of Anchorage home, rough weather slowed us down. When the weather finally cleared for a moment, we raced through the waves to get to the tunnel before it closed. At that speed, the tender boat lurched and pitched through the water, tossing me violently around the boat. It sent my stomach churning, too. In all my years of fishing, that was the only time I ever felt even remotely seasick. It was a wild ride!

Several years ago, the president of our company also asked me if I would go aboard as a chef on our CEO's yacht and cook for him and his guests for the last week of yachting season. I objected at first, saying I was a boat cook, not a chef! But somehow, he talked me into it. Part of my job was to provision the galley. So, off to Costco I went. I had no idea what kind of food to buy. I was a fishing boat cook. I had never "plated" a dish in my life! But our CEO met me on the yacht to show me around. It was a beautiful boat – all shiny and golden. I was more terrified boarding that yacht than I'd ever been in the fishing business. The reason they needed me so suddenly was their chef had died quite unexpectedly. Apparently yacht crews generally drink and party when the owners are not on board. Unfortunately for this young chef, during one of these debaucheries, he fell off the dock and drowned.

As we motored through the Ballard Locks with our crew of four, I had a glimpse of how rich people must feel as people on shore stared at us transiting through the locks. Owners of yachts of this size and class usually fly to where their boat is moored. In this case, its home port was Friday Harbor in the San Juan Islands, Washington, where the guests and owners would be waiting for us. The accommodations for crew were very tight.

We arrived in Friday Harbor and had the task of getting the boat ready for the guests and owners. Since all the crew who had been aboard during the accident had been fired, excepting the captain, we had a new crew sailing with us. I'd had the chance to query a Steward who'd been working on yachts for many years about the dos and don'ts of cooking on a yacht. But I was still feeling some apprehension.

The next morning, a little grey skiff came puttering over to the yacht and a small man with a scruffy beard and sloppy shorts tried to come aboard. He seemed inebriated, so I asked if I could help him. He said that he was looking for the man who owned the yacht, my CEO. The guy had a very thick British accent, so it was difficult to understand him. Plus, with his disheveled appearance, he looked like a "wharf rat" and not someone who should be coming aboard. I explained in my most polite manner that the owner was not aboard and not expected until the following day. To which, he said, "okay" - and walked away.

The next day, we had a lot of guests arrive for dinner. Imagine my surprise to see this guy come sauntering up the gangway, very nicely dressed, with a beautiful blond woman on his arm. I didn't recognize him as the guy I'd stopped from getting on the boat the day before at first. I was just looking at him and as he started exclaiming how he already knew me from the day before, I realized he was the guy I'd thought looked like a "wharf rat." The woman on her arm was his lovely wife, Gigi, and she introduced her husband as Alan. She laughed when I told her I'd thought he was a bum on the docks and said, "Yep, he cleans up well." It turns out my "wharf rat" was Alan White, the well-known drummer from the famous band, Yes!

I worked on that yacht for over a week. It was a wonderful experience – and, I learned a lot, including how to set a proper table and how to plate food. Yes, they do iron the sheets on luxury yachts! It was really something to see how the "other half" lives. More recently, there is a new reality show on TV called "Below the Decks." It has been fun to watch and made me realize just how inexperienced I was when I set foot on that yacht. I made so many mistakes. But, thankfully most of the guests were people I knew from my industry. So, it went well even though I was clearly "out of my element." The first meal I cooked was a pot roast. The CEOs wife came into the galley and took a photo of it, exclaiming that "they'd never had a pot roast on the yacht!" It was a different world, folks.

On August 15, 2019, I traveled north on the *Katie Ann* again to train a newbie one-on-one. With my new job description and a significant raise in pay, I had been asked to sail on the *Katie Ann* to Dutch Harbor with a new steward the company had hired. I felt it would be a great opportunity for me to give this steward a good launching into the world of American Seafood Company. She had a very impressive resume. Going back on the *Katie Ann* was so nostalgic for me. I have very fond memories of my time sailing on the

Katie Ann, but also some very painful ones. This was the vessel that I was working on when Rick Black, the observer on the boat, astutely predicted that I would be the future Mrs. John Entenmann. This was also the vessel where John had his accident and nearly lost his arm. So, I had a week to reflect on my life and where I'd been then and where I was now. These memories all came flooding back to me as I boarded the boat.

My trainee had never backloaded a boat. I steamed along with her to Dutch Harbor to be sure everything went okay. I met a new Captain, Leif Ericksen (really!), aka Brandon, as I affectionately called him. He was a great captain and I enjoyed sailing with him. He was very relaxed, easy to talk to, and really cared about the crew and boat. I often commented on how much fun we would have had sailing together back in the day. He is as close to "old school" as you can get without crossing the line. We also had a brand-new purser who was sailing for the first time with our company. So, he had a lot to learn, but I believe he was up to the challenge. Also sailing with us was Lance, the training guy, who was also new to our company. He had no fishing boat experience. So, he steamed on the *Katie Ann* to observe how our boats operate and to help guide him in his new job. We had many brainstorming meetings with crew from the top of the boat to the bottom. We shared a lot of information and ideas to make life more pleasant on our boats. A lot of good ideas came from that week-long steam.

The galley on this boat had gone through several Chief Stewards in the last few years and needed some love. It was my job to "fix" problems in the galley. Ava, the new steward, was delightful. I believed she would be a great fit for our galleys, whether she stayed on the *Katie Ann* or moved to another boat. She had a very calming demeanor and presence. She cared about crew and welcomed any suggestions or comments from others. It was a very good sign, in my opinion. She was very approachable.

The poor *Katie Ann* had been woefully neglected in the past few years. An entire season would be needed to clean her up so that she can look as good as possible for an old ship. I had a brand-new housekeeper who had never been on a boat. Her name was CJ. From what I could see, she would be a very good fit for the *Katie Ann*. The standard housekeeper was coming back after one trip and probably wouldn't be happy with the instructions I left with Ava to get the boat back on track. The improvements meant a lot more work was ahead for them, but I believed that they were off to a good start for the *Katie Ann*.

As I fell asleep at night, I reminisced on those long-ago wild days on *Katie Ann*. Waking in the morning, I gazed again out my porthole to a familiar, well-loved, long-remembered view. As the sun inched slowly above the horizon and early morning pink and orange light danced across that magnificent dark-blue seascape reaching as far as my eyes can see, I felt that tranquility again and breathed in a deep feeling of peace as I fell asleep, rocked slightly by the summer's gentle waves.

The next Thursday morning, we steamed into Dutch Harbor. Lance and I finished our jobs, got into the truck and headed to the airport. The weather was foggy, so our flights out did not look promising. But, as in the past and no doubt in the future, if a plane gets in, one can always get out. Since we were delayed, Lance and I had the chance to spend a day driving all over Unalaska and Dutch Harbor to see the sights. We drove out to the rugged, craggy shoreline of Summers Bay. Its rolling green hills were covered with wildflowers, with a hint of fall hanging crisp in the air. Pounding waves entered the snow-tinged bay, lapping against the ocean-like shore. We had a splendid day! We finally got the word that all flights were cancelled, which was typical of Dutch Harbor. So, we checked into a hotel. The office continued trying to get us on a cargo charter that was supposed to land in Dutch Harbor at around 5:30 P.M. ACE Cargo called us and told us to get to the airport and that the plane was attempting to land....which it did.

While sitting at the airport, I recognized a man and woman also sitting there. It was Bob and Shirley Marquette from my very early days of fishing. I had not seen them since the early 1990s. They were our expeditors, the people who monitored our workflow when I worked on the *Saga Sea*. It was curious to run into them in Dutch Harbor after all that time. We had a nice catch up on the past 28 years. When the cargo plane landed, cargo and several crew members for our company were off-loaded. Lance and I got the last two seats on the flight out.

When I was on board the *Katie Ann*, all seemed to go well. But when I got home, a flurry of emails flooded my computer. As soon as I left, the old timers started to push back on the new procedures. Apparently, the boat needed some stability.

Those long months of fishing in the Bering Sea in Alaska are over. But I am still working in boat galleys and connected to that life. It's interesting to be the Relief Chief Steward for numerous boats. Each galley is different and a new adventure in cooking always awaits me. Today, you could say I have one foot out the door. I'm nearing retirement age and am ready to retire. Another birthday has just come and gone, and I am now 68 years young. I'm still enjoying my new job and hope that I can make a difference. I believe that change is in the air. I don't know how many more years I will be doing this job, but I have a new challenge with this new job description. I will still be cooking in port and when the season is over, I look forward to doing that. This is my real connection – to cook for those hungry men and women during shipyard layovers who are just happy to be there, with very few complaints. I've also trained a support team who can bring the galleys up to snuff since some of the boat galleys really need the help. I feel I've left a good legacy. Being in the industry has given me so many wonderful experiences. I have met great people who I am proud to call my friends. There are still some that never got over dealing with me. I'm a strong, independent thinker! But if a person is to survive in the fishing environment, they must be strong. I stepped on a lot of toes, cried myself to sleep many nights rolling around on the Bering Sea, but I believe that's what made me who I am today.

Heading out on a skiff with Trish for a hike in Prince William Sound.

Transport to *Katie Ann* via small float plane, Prince William Sound.

Block of ice from the glacier, Prince William Sound.

View from my porthole.

Trish, Jazz, and Mate Mark at Prince William Sound.

Though this photo was taken at Prince Willian Sound, diving into the frigid water in the Bering Sea and at Dutch Harbor and Prince William Sound was a "right-of-passage" that signaled the beginning of a good fishing season.

Jazz and the girls in Prince William Sound after they jumped into the water.

Trish on the *Katie Ann* cooking with a flourish.

Trish using pot in the *Katie Ann* galley to build muscle.

In all the years I fished, this was the only time I was hoisted down the side of a boat in a skiff. I was being hoisted from the deck of one fishing vessel, the *Jaeger*, to the other, the *Eagle*.

It was scary! As I was lowered in the skiff, the motion caused it to slam repeatedly against the side of the boat - and then it slammed again as the skiff was lifted into the second boat. It was quite an experience!

Preparing to hoist the skiff up the side of the vessel to pick me up.

The skiff that carried me from one vessel to another.

Preparing to hoist the skiff up the side of the vessel to pick me up.

The waves were choppy the day I was transported by skiff from one boat to another.

Bosun Karre, the skiff driver.

Aboard the skiff ride in the Bering Sea.

Hiking at Prince William Sound, Alaska.

Trish hiking in Prince William Sound, Alaska.

On the *Katie Ann*, bosun Ozzie, a deckhand, Trish and I got into big trouble. We went on a hike (pictured above) and stayed out until after the sun went down. It caused quite a stir and had the entire tender fleet looking for us. They were certain we'd been eaten by bears!

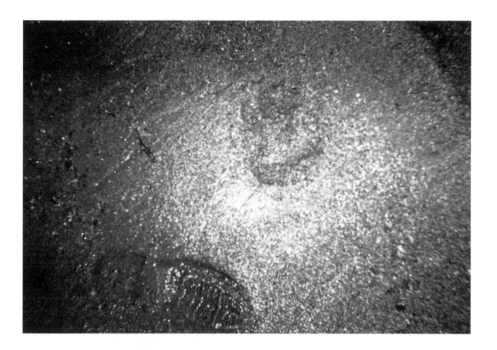

Bear prints, Prince William Sound, Alaska.

Sindi with Rande Bodal aboard the luxury yacht, the *American Pride* in Friday Harbor, WA. Rande is the mother of my then CEO, who hired me to cook on his yacht. I'm seen here in the galley of the yacht.

Svin Vik, factory manager, Sindi, and Captain Skippy.

A glacier in the background, Prince William Sound. Breathtaking!

Captain Jens on the *Northern Eagle.*

Dewey, Captain of the *Bering Star.*

Dewey, me, Trish, and the *Bering Star* deck hands. Dewey came over to the *Katie Ann* from his boat the *Bering Sea* to invite us over for dinner on their boat, Prince William Sound.

Sailing Forward

Today, I have a much bigger challenge. Just as I have stuck one foot out the back door toward retirement, American Seafoods has offered me an opportunity to work closely with the vessels and our Human Resources department as a Fleet Galley Advisor. In conjunction with the vessel galley staff, I will assist with budgeting, ordering, and tracking inventory, and support HR in hiring and training galley staff. In short, I will be a resource point for all galley matters, as well as overseeing staff rotations and food safety/health. Also, while vessels are in port, I will be responsible for galley operations and the preparation of daily lunches for the crew. Again, I will be out to sea as needed to assist, train, and fill in for galley staff. With the full support of the office, we are hopefully going to be able to guide our aging out crew members into retirement and guide our up-and-coming young crew to take on this daunting task of being successful. We have paved the way.

Nonetheless, when Covid-19 struck American Seafoods and our world, every plan I made with HR shifted. I had no idea just how much my work with the vessels would change. In addition to guiding our young crew into becoming successful and providing support to our retirees, what I did for the company dramatically changed overnight.

Covid 19 hit during the height of our hake season in Fall 2019. As we attempted to off-load our fish at Bellingham cold storage, we were blocked from coming onto the dock. Bellingham cold storage was where we normally off-loaded our fish, but that day was different. Covid-19 had spread through our boats, and we had so many cases, we were not allowed to even come on the dock, much less off-load our product.

Then, because our Covid numbers were so high, the Center for Disease Control tied up three of our vessels in Seattle. They had no idea what to do with them, so we kept all our crews onboard the vessels until CDC could figure out how to quarantine them and keep them safe. Ultimately, CDC concluded that after fourteen days of isolation, the virus could not be transmitted, even if someone tested positive. However, it would be weeks of waiting onboard the vessels before they made that determination.

Once we knew that 14-day quarantines on land would be necessary, with the intention of streamlining our quarantine and making it run more efficiently, we hired a quarantine manager through American Seafoods. However, the guy sold us a bill of goods and ran roughshod over our company. He made multiple bad decisions, posturing himself as an authority when he was far from it. People in our company said "You should contact John Lee, our purchasing manager, or contact Sindi, who has cooked for these people for 25+ years. They can help you." But this guy said, "Oh, no. I've got this." Nobody saw the red flag. I do not know how many multi-millions of wasted dollars he cost the company, but it was a lot.

For that first full quarantine, we had six hotels: two in Redmond, one in Bellevue, and three in Seattle. It was a proverbial shitshow - I felt so bad for our crews. Our new quarantine manager was telling the hotels to not serve healthy foods like salad or fish. Plus, when the crews arrived at their various hotels – every crew had a different hotel – they checked in but there were absolutely no snacks for them. They were locked in their rooms with nothing to eat. It was horrific.

To mitigate the confusion, the company hired me to work our second quarantine alongside the quarantine manager. It was immediately clear to me that this guy had no clue what he was doing. All our crews were quarantined, locked up in their rooms, but what little food they were getting was horrendous. This guy just did not care about them.

After the quarantine manager was hired, I stayed in one of the hotels to help process the crews. They would show up, their luggage would be searched, and if they had alcohol, we would take it out. We would then get them checked in, they would have a Covid test and then be escorted up to their rooms. They would have to stay in their rooms for 14 days in solitary confinement. Each day, they were given a list of snack options. However, we could not provide the snack options because our quarantine manager had not ordered any. It was atrocious!

At this point, I just took over and started ordering snacks and water during the day. However, the hotel food was still horrendous. Ultimately, I got kicked out of the hotel kitchen because although the banquet chef said she was open to my suggestions, as soon as I gave them to her, she said, "I do not want her back here." We did not have an option. Bad food was apparently going to stay on the quarantine manager's agenda.

At first, due to security, the company was not allowing Uber Eats or Door Dash. However, I talked to my boss and pushed it through that if the crews did not like the food they were being served, they could order out. Our purchasing manager, John Lee, and I collaborated to bring snacks to our crews. Then everyone was all hands-on deck, from CEOs to an assistant and a processor. We were all out running around getting snacks for the crews in all those different hotels. It did not matter who you were or what you did, everyone in our organization had a quarantine hat on.

We ended up getting everyone out and onto the boats. But everything had to be fumigated. Luggage had to come out of the rooms the day before the crews left. It was loaded into big semi-trucks and driven down to the pier where it was fumigated.

The following day, our crews were taken out of their rooms in increments of ten people, (because we were all in a little bubble). They were taken down to the pier, where they collected their luggage, got on the boat, and were good to go. Any of those people who were positive would end up in another hotel where they stayed for 10 days and got tested again. If they tested positive after 10 days, they were still considered good to go and sent off to their boats. It was assumed they would not contaminate anyone at that point.

Last year, once people were hired, we sent them to a quarantine hotel in Anchorage, Alaska, and that is where they stayed for 14-days. When their boats came into Dutch Harbor, we had to charter a plane to get them from Anchorage to Dutch Harbor. We were also flying people up to Dutch Harbor directly. Sometimes the boats would go to Cold Bay, stop fishing, and go pick up crew. However, if the fishing was good, we were not going to go pick up crew because "we were on the fish now." This meant that sometimes crews were in quarantine in Anchorage for days. One guy I knew was locked up in his room for 29 days! The only time they could go out was for a smoke or to exercise. There were designated areas for both, just outside their rooms. However, in winter it is bitter cold in Anchorage, so the conditions for going outside at all were not ideal.

Meanwhile, the quarantine manager had been given him a corporate card and since he fancied himself a know-it-all who knew everyone and how to do everything, he made some extremely poor purchases. He ordered 150 microwave ovens and probably 100 apartment-sized refrigerators that he was going to give to the hotels. Why? Our crews could not leave their rooms to go out and shop for food to store in the refrigerators or cook in the microwaves. It would have been far better to spend that money on providing them with better food! The fact is this guy did not know anything. Our warehouse was full of stacks of unused microwave ovens and refrigerators. I do not know how he got away with that. But shortly after the end of the last quarantine, he got fired. I wish I could have been a fly on the wall for that one!

However, we did have some good people. Lance, our training guy, from American Seafoods, was instrumental in getting that quarantine up to snuff to what it should be so that crews had healthy snacks to eat. He helped tremendously. The hotel food was still questionable but at least Lance provided them with some healthy food.

That is how we did it last year. This year, after we got everyone off out of Seattle, each boat was finally allowed one rotation. Normally, boats are allowed three to four rotations, which means that crews come off the boat and other crews are allowed to take their place – and while only one rotation was not ideal, when we had no rotations, crews were exhausted.

This year, everything was an entirely different scenario. We only had three hotels and the quarantine ran like a well-oiled machine. All the right people were in the right places with the right stuff was waiting for crews when they arrived. We had very few glitches. Plus, out of 800 employees, we only had four positives, and they were all asymptomatic, so we quarantined them in Seattle. The key crew that lived locally and had two vaccinations were allowed to quarantine at home for seven days. On the day before they were due to fly, they would then come to one of the hotels, take a Covid test, stay overnight, and then get on a charter in the middle of the night at Boeing field and fly to Anchorage and on to Dutch Harbor. If the processors were double vaccinated, they were allowed to quarantine only seven days in the hotel. If they had only one vaccination, they had to quarantine for 14-days. In that case, they would get their second vaccination at the hotel. Those who were not vaccinated got both vaccination shots at the hotel. The process ran beautifully.

Also, every hotel we were contracting with was providing the food, so we did not have to have catered meals. The hotels sent me the menus for breakfast, lunch, and dinner for seven-day menus and I got to go through every single menu and say "yes, or no, let us add more of this to it or less of this." That was an incredible improvement for the crews, with few complaints from them except for two weeks when we had to order in from the outside since the hotels were getting busier. Covid restrictions were opening so the hotels started getting busy. A year ago, they had been begging us for their business but now we had so many people in their hotel – and they had their own customers – that they could not provide food for all our 150 people. We had to have their food catered in and it was substandard quality. As soon as I found out about that debacle, I did something about it. You cannot fix it if you do not know about it! Our crews are a lot happier about the overall quarantine experience this year.

We just shut down our last quarantine. We have one more starting on the 26th but it should go well because we are now approaching the end of quarantining for Covid-19. We are glad to see the quarantine lift because the entire experience dealing with Covid-19 was horrendous for the company. Nobody knew what to expect. It was all such unfamiliar territory. Even when our six boats were sitting at the dock at the end of the season, we had a guard shack at the end of every boat. If you were an American Seafoods employee, you had to get on a list, go to a trailer where your temperature would be taken immediately by state-of-the-art equipment, and be issued an automatic tag with your name printed on it. Then you would take your new ID tag to the guard station positioned at the end of your boat, and the guard would check to see that your name was on the list. Only then would you be issued a wristband. If you were a vendor, people who come on the boat to fix them, you would need to prove that you had a recent negative

Covid test result before we would allow you on our boats. It was crazy. Can you imagine the money spent in this process? We had to provide food for the shipyard people as well as numerous vendors. Typically, when I am down on the boat, I am just cooking for our people. However, since I had to provide food for our people as well as countless shipyard workers and vendors, I had to find adequate food trucks to go down to the docks and feed these guys three times a day. This was a challenge in and of itself, and extremely expensive. But what other option did we have? That is how we fed them for the last two years.

The Covid-19 impact must be improving because I was down at the pier this morning and Luci, our all-around timecard gal, was there too. Last year, she was so paranoid that she wore a hat, mask, and gloves all the time. Today, for the first time, I saw her beautiful smile again! She wore no hat, mask, or gloves.

Grant, a great guy who is now the quarantine manager, is doing a fine job. He was recently invoicing for the quarantine and the bills were in the millions – and that is just for 2021, this year. I cannot begin to imagine what it cost last year with our previous quarantine manager. The costs have been staggering due to providing crews with food, housing them in hotels until they are fit for duty, sending a nurse by their door every day for a wellness check, and having to use security and cameras throughout the hotels to be sure of their compliance. Without meaning to, people can unwittingly break their quarantine. For example, someone in quarantine may be outside smoking and need a light. At that moment, someone else walks by and offers that person a lighter. The automatic response would be to put ones' hand out and let someone else put a lighter in it. That is normal smokers' behavior. But that is a big no-no in quarantine! Equally, a friend wanting to accommodate a 14-day isolation might drop off a pack of cigarettes to someone in quarantine. That is also a no-no because crews are all supposed to stay in their own little bubble with no contact from the outside world. That is where we try to keep them. It was much more successful this year because the right people were doing the jobs. Thankfully at this writing, it appears Covid-19 quarantining is behind us. Our expenses should start to even out. Right now, though the fishing is slow and somewhat poor because of warming weather, this trend can shift quickly because fishing is fishing.

Some days are good, some are bad – that is why they call it fishing!

When asked if I would recommend that a young woman go into the fishing industry, my initial answer was an emphatic "no." The work has been extremely strenuous and the constant clambering for equal rights and respect dealt hard emotional blows on my spirit. Fishing is not a work for the faint of heart and required enormous stamina. I had to fight constantly to "thicken my skin" for the onslaught. For as exciting and unique as it is, it is a highly demanding work that takes everything you can give and then asks for more. My entire body ached all the time, particularly my feet and my heart hurt more than once. It was also work that claimed lives. It's sobering to think that twenty of the people I worked with have since died of alcoholism, substance abuse, heart attack or by accident. In fact, we just lost two young stewards this week, Jeff Byrd and George Farrow. Jeff was a great cook and friend. It was a sad day when he passed. All of our galley crew and stewards, current and past, showed up for his memorial. He touched a lot of lives. It makes me feel sad and nostalgic. Fishing was a rough life.

On reflection, however, I've changed my mind. Those of us who fought those equality fights in the early days really paved the way for future generations of women in fishing. I realize it's a different world for women now in every industry. More protections are in place for us in the workforce, even those industries where there are far more men than women that have classically been thought of as "a man's world." Most of the equality battles have been won, even out to sea. So, for those strong, beautiful Sisters of the Sea (SOS) women, I'd recommend they challenge themselves and work hard so they can advance. Be the strongest they can be and don't take any nonsense without speaking out about it. The hardships of the past have been softened by the women who came before them and pressed our way through the malaise of testosterone-fueled atmospheres and male egos. That said, old habits die hard and the boundaries of what's appropriate can still be fuzzy. Just days ago, I was laughing in conversation with a fellow officer who knows full well that I'm married. Yet as I walked away from him, he grabbed my bottom and gave it a tight squeeze. I jumped, but since I was long ago conditioned to ignore this type of banter, I shook it off. I know in some ways he will always see me as "one of the guys" which gives him the liberty to think that's okay. I also like having a sense of comradery with my crewmates and that's important at sea. However, it did give me cause to ponder that even though the rules have changed, some of those past behaviors still linger.

I don't regret working in the fishing industry. I wanted adventure and I certainly got plenty of it. Plus, it was an experience that built character and resilience. But now, aside from taking those occasional short trips north and working my day job cooking for crew on fishing boats dockside, I am free to go home at night and attend to my true loves: John, my dog, and my vegetable and flower gardens. John and I have time to travel in our RV, see friends, and relax. And, I must admit, while it's not seen through a porthole, that view I see is beyond wonderful.

Porthole view of Seattle's Pier 90 from the *Northern Eagle.*

My grandson, Keoni, always helps out in the galley during shipyard. This time he made it on the safety card for the fleet.

Sunset, Prince William Sound.

Me and "tornado" Cass touring around the   Mount Shishaldin blowing ash, Alaska,
Amaknak Island in Unalaska, Alaska.   January 2020.

ACKNOWLEDGMENTS

I would like to give a heartfelt thank you to Judy Schiffner's never-ending support of me in the efforts to write this book. She saved years of emails and mailed them to me after she met me. She also never gave up on encouraging me to write this book. I'd also like to recognize all my Brothers and Sisters of the Sea who have passed away to that "big ocean in the sky." Without the experiences I had with them, I could not have written this book. There are far too many of them to acknowledge individually, but I will mention a few who stand out in my mind. John Bloomfield, Chief Steward and my first boss, was instrumental in introducing me to work in the galley of a commercial fishing vessel. He was also a cherished friend. Captain John Szymzak, also my boss, was very encouraging of me and my work. Two foremen, Walley Chiplock and Terry Sutton were very supportive in helping me learn "the ropes" of commercial fishing. Galley Steward and First Cook Jeff Byrd was great to cook with, as well as galley crewmates George Farrow, Darius, and Howard Dietrich. I would like to thank American Seafood for the many years of employment. The company has been very supportive and helpful in my journey to get this book done. So many to thank. Finally, a special thank you goes to writer/editor Catherine Lenox who spent countless hours sorting through my journals, notes, clippings, and memos to help me shape this book. Her belief in the value of my story and her talent for helping me tell it cannot be underestimated. She is awesome!

ABOUT THE AUTHOR

Sindi Giancoli spent twenty-five years as a Chief Steward for American Seafoods Company and other commercial fishing companies in Alaska and the Bering Sea. She lives in Woodinville, Washington with her husband John Entenmann and dog, Daisy. *Woman's View from a Porthole* is her first book.

www.WomansViewFromAPorthole.com

Sindi holding a King Salmon during her days on the ship *Claymore Sea*.